Lectures in

Austen Baraza Omonyo

Lectures in Project Monitoring & Evaluation

For Professional Practitioners

LAP LAMBERT Academic Publishing

Impressum / Imprint

Bibliografische Information der Deutschen Nationalbibliothek: Die Deutsche Nationalbibliothek verzeichnet diese Publikation in der Deutschen Nationalbibliografie; detaillierte bibliografische Daten sind im Internet über http://dnb.d-nb.de abrufbar.

Alle in diesem Buch genannten Marken und Produktnamen unterliegen warenzeichen-, marken- oder patentrechtlichem Schutz bzw. sind Warenzeichen oder eingetragene Warenzeichen der jeweiligen Inhaber. Die Wiedergabe von Marken, Produktnamen, Gebrauchsnamen, Handelsnamen, Warenbezeichnungen u.s.w. in diesem Werk berechtigt auch ohne besondere Kennzeichnung nicht zu der Annahme, dass solche Namen im Sinne der Warenzeichen- und Markenschutzgesetzgebung als frei zu betrachten wären und daher von jedermann benutzt werden dürften.

Bibliographic information published by the Deutsche Nationalbibliothek: The Deutsche Nationalbibliothek lists this publication in the Deutsche Nationalbibliografie; detailed bibliographic data are available in the Internet at http://dnb.d-nb.de.

Any brand names and product names mentioned in this book are subject to trademark, brand or patent protection and are trademarks or registered trademarks of their respective holders. The use of brand names, product names, common names, trade names, product descriptions etc. even without a particular marking in this work is in no way to be construed to mean that such names may be regarded as unrestricted in respect of trademark and brand protection legislation and could thus be used by anyone.

Coverbild / Cover image: www.ingimage.com

Verlag / Publisher:
LAP LAMBERT Academic Publishing
ist ein Imprint der / is a trademark of
OmniScriptum GmbH & Co. KG
Heinrich-Böcking-Str. 6-8, 66121 Saarbrücken, Deutschland / Germany
Email: info@lap-publishing.com

Herstellung: siehe letzte Seite /
Printed at: see last page
ISBN: 978-3-659-62815-3

LECTURES IN PROJECT MONITORING AND EVALUATION FOR PROFESSIONAL PRACTITIONERS

BY

OmonyoAusten Baraza

© BarazaOmonyo

Lectures in Project Monitoring and Evaluation for Professional Practitioners

ISBN: 978-3-659-62815-3

First Published 2015

Published in 2015 by Lambert Academic Publishing

ACKNOWLEDGEMENT

This book is a result of many years of practice, compilation and research. I am indebted to the Centre for Finance and Project Management™ (CFPM), a Project Management training and consultancy firm based in Nairobi, Kenya, for giving me the opportunity and platform against which I have written this book. The book compiles the lectures that I have delivered at the Centre for Finance and Project Management ™ in the areas of Project Management, Monitoring and Evaluation. CFPM was the first PMI Registered Education Provider in Kenya and has successfully prepared very many professionals for the PMI certifications across East Africa.

The reader will notice that this book draws heavily on PMI publications such as the *PMBOK® Guide* and Standards. The book also refers extensively to the UK Government official Project Management Methodology-PRINCE2®. This book also draws from findings based on extensive consultancy work that I have been involved in while working at the CFPM. Finally, I am grateful to staff at the CFPM for their invaluable contribution to making this book a success.

TABLE OF CONTENTS

Contents

vi

LIST OF TABLES

LIST OF FIGURES

To The Almighty God and My Family

PART I: INTRODUCTION TO PROJECT MANAGEMENT, MONITORING AND EVALUATION

LECTURE ONE: INTRODUCTION TO PROJECT MANAGEMENT
Lecture Outline

1.1 Introduction
1.2 Lecture Objectives
1.3 Definition and characteristics of projects
1.4 Measures of project success
1.5 Characteristics of successful project managers
1.6 Project management processes
1.7 Summary
1.8 Self-test
1.9 References and suggestions for further reading

1.1 Introduction

This lecture is meant to introduce you to the discipline of Project Management by providing key elements that are necessary to aid in the process of Monitoring and Evaluating Project Management practices. Many people claiming to be experts in the area of Project Monitoring and Evaluation have no background knowledge in the subject of Project Management. This affects the practicality of the recommendations they make and the processes they follow since you cannot effectively monitor and evaluate projects without understanding their logic. In modern day Project Monitoring and Evaluation, you are often required to comment on the process of project management covering initiation through to closure. There is no way you will fulfill this term of reference if you have no idea of what standard activities are performed in each project process.

1.2 Lecture Objectives

1. Define and characterize projects

2. Distinguish projects from operations, programs and portfolios

3. Define the role of a project manager and characterize project management success

4. Use a processual approach to understand the scope of the discipline of Project Management.

1.3 Definition and Characteristics of Projects

Various writers on the subject of Project Management have varied ways of defining Projects. It is important to note that the circumstances of the time play a major role in determining which definition suits where. Some of these definitions are presented below:

Harrison (1985):	A project is a non-routine or non-repetitive, one-off undertaking; normally which has discrete time, financial and technical performance goals.
Buchanan & Body (1992):	A project is a unique venture with a beginning and an end; conducted by people to meet established goals, schedule and quality.
Turner (1993):	A project is an endeavour in which human (or machine), material and financial resources are organized in a novel way, to undertake a unique scope work, of given specification, within constraints of cost and time, so as to deliver beneficial change defined by quantitative and qualitative objectives.
Nigel, et. al, (1998):	A project is a set of activities which have a defined start point and a defined end point state, pursue a defined goal and use a defined set of resources.
British Standards Institute:	A project is a unique set of coordinated activities with a definite start and finishing point, undertaken by an individual or organization to meet specific objectives within defined, scheduled cost and performance parameters.
Kerzner (2008):	A project is any series of activities and tasks that have a specific objective to be completed within certain circumstances, have a defined start and end dates, have funding limits if applicable, consume human and non-human resources, and are multifunctional i.e. cut across several functional lines.
PRINCE2® (2009):	A project is a temporary organization that is created for the purpose of delivering one or more business products according to an agreed Business Case
ISO 21500 (2012):	A project is a unique set of processes consisting of coordinated and controlled activities with start and finish dates, undertaken to achieve an objective.
PMBOK® Guide (2013):	A project is a temporary endeavor undertaken to create unique products, services or results.

Table 1.1: Definitions of "Project"

All the definitions listed above have some elements in common. These common elements form the characteristics of a project, which help us to understand the nature of projects and therefore project monitoring and evaluation. The elements are presented below:

3

- **An objective** - a definable result, output or product that is typically defined in terms of the cost, the quality, timing and benefits of the output from the Project activities.
- **Complexity** - many different tasks are required to be undertaken to achieve a project's objectives. The relationship between all these tasks can be complex, especially when the number of separate tasks in the project is large.
- **Uniqueness-** A project is usually a "one-off" not a repetitive undertaking. Even repeat projects such as the construction of another chemical plant to the same specification, will have distinctive differences in terms of resources used and the actual environment in which the project takes place.
- **Uncertainty** - All projects are planned before they are executed and therefore carry an element of risk.
- **Temporary nature** - projects have a defined beginning and end, so a temporary concentration of resources is needed to carry out the undertaking.
- **Life Cycle** - The resource needs for a Project change during the course of its life cycle. The typical pattern of resource needs for a project follow a predictable path.

These elements serve to distinguish projects from other types of operation. They also serve to distinguish projects from programs and portfolios. Whereas operations are ongoing activities that are routine in nature, projects have a defined beginning and an end. A program is a group of related projects, subprograms, and program activities, managed in a coordinated way to obtain benefits not available from managing them individually. All projects within programs are related through a common goal, often of strategic importance to sponsoring organization. If projects have separate goals, are not characterized by synergistic benefit delivery, and are only related by common funding, technology, or stakeholders, then these efforts are better managed as a portfolio rather than as a program.

The table below adapted from the *PMBOK® Guide* (2013), presents a comparative overview of Projects, Programs and Portfolios.

4

	PROJECTS	PROGRAMS	PORTFOLIOS
Scope	Projects have defined objectives. Scope is progressively elaborated throughout the project life cycle.	Programs have a large scope and provide more significant benefits.	Portfolios have a business scope that changes with the strategic goals of the organization.
Change	Project managers expect change and implement processes to keep change managed and controlled.	The program manager must expect change from both inside and outside the program and be prepared for it.	Portfolio managers continually monitor changes in the broad environment.
Planning	Project managers progressively elaborate high-level information into detailed plans throughout the project life cycle.	Program managers develop the overall program plan and create high-level plans to guide detailed planning at the component level.	Portfolio managers create and maintain necessary processes and communication relative to the aggregate portfolio.
Management	Project managers manage the project team to meet the project objectives.	Program managers manage the program staff and the project managers; they provide vision and overall leadership.	Portfolio managers may manage or coordinate portfolio management staff.
Success	Success is measured by product and project quality, timeliness budget compliance, and degree of customer satisfaction.	Success is measured by the degree to which the program satisfies the needs and benefits for which it was undertaken.	Success is measured in terms of aggregate performance of portfolio components.
Monitoring	Project managers monitor and control the work producing the products, services, or results that the project was undertaken to produce.	Program managers monitor the progress of program components to ensure the overall goals, schedules, budget and benefits of the program will be met.	Portfolio managers monitor aggregate performance and value indicators.

Table 1.2: comparative overview of Projects, Programs and Portfolios

1.4 Measures of Project Success

All the definitions of a "project" presented earlier in this chapter showed that every project has an objective. Attainment of this objective is the primary concern of project monitoring and evaluation and is the ultimate measure of project success. According to Turner (2007), project success refers to the criteria, both qualitative and quantitative, against which a project is judged to be successful. Generally, the criteria used to evaluate project success are based on stakeholders' particular expectations of the project (Jiang,

Stakeholders!

(Chen, & Klein, 2002) with success reflecting the extent to which these expectations are perceived to have been met. Various researchers have considered the question of what constitutes project success. In Table 1.3below, we summarize the main metrics that define project success categorized by researcher/author:

Author (s)/Researcher(s)	Success Measures Advanced
Cleland & Ireland (2002):	Time, Cost, Quality
Pinto &Slevin (1988); Barker, Pinto &Rouhiainen (2001):	Time, Cost, Quality, Customer Satisfaction
De Wit (1988):	Budget Performance, Schedule Performance, Client Satisfaction, Functionality, Contractor Satisfaction, Project Manager/Team Satisfaction
Lim & Mohamed (1999):	Completion, User Satisfaction
Freeman & Beale (1992):	Technical Performance, Efficiency of Execution, Customer Satisfaction, Personal Growth, Manufacturability & Business Performance
Turner, Zolin, &Remmington (2009):	Project Output, Project Outcome& Impact
Wateridge (1995)	Commercial Success, Meet User Requirements, Meet Budget, Happy Users, Achieve Purpose, Meet Timescales, Happy Sponsor, Meet Quality, Happy Team
Shenhar, Dvir, & Levy (1997); Shenhar, Dvir, Levy &Maltz (2001); Shenhar&Dvir (2007); Hoegl&Gemuenden (2000):	Project Efficiency, Impact on Team, Impact on the Customer, Business Success, Preparing for the future
Kerzner (2008):	Within the allocated time period, Within the budgeted cost, At the proper performance or specification level, With acceptance by the customer/user, With minimum or mutually agreed upon scope changes, Without disturbing the main workflow of the organization, Without changing the corporate culture

Table 1.3: Project Success Measures

Based on our synthesis we categorize these success measures into three dimensions namely:

a)   Those that enhance the project's operational excellence (traditionally referred to as "iron triangle")-cost, time, quality.

b)   Those that enhance the project's strategic focus-scope control, benefits realization

c)   Those that ensure inspired leadership on the project-risk management, team leadership and stakeholder engagement

6

This categorization is consistent with the six project performance metrics suggested by the PRINCE2® methodology-cost, timescale, quality, scope, risk and benefits. Risk management, team leadership and stakeholder engagement are seen as contextual factors that enhance Project Delivery Capability (PDC). In practice, these performance metrics provide a sufficient framework on which monitoring and evaluation of project success is anchored.

Ordinarily, unsuccessful project exhibit the following failures:

- Design and definition failures where the scope of the program and/or project(s) are not clearly defined and required outcomes and /or outputs are not described with sufficient clarity.
- Decision making failures due to inadequate level of sponsorship and commitment to the program and / or project(s), i.e. there is no person in authority able to resolve issues.
- Program and Project discipline failures, including weak arrangements for managing risks and inability to manage change in requirements.
- Supplier management failures, including lack of understanding of supplier commercial imperatives, poor contractual set-up and management.
- People failure, including disconnect between the program and / or project(s) and stakeholders, lack of ownership, cultural issues.

Explain how and why the environment in which a project is implemented can determine its success

The roles and responsibilities of the Project Manager ...

1.5 Characteristics of successful Project Managers

In order to deliver a project successfully, and in order to co-ordinate the efforts of many people in different parts within and outside of the organization all projects need a Project Manager. The role of the Manager is to achieve the project objectives. They do this by planning and controlling the project from initiation to closure, trying to bring order to complexity and reducing the level of uncertainty. Many of a Project Manager's activities are concerned with managing human resources. Project Managers also need to procure all the resources for the Project. They are also concerned with controlling uncertainty by forecasting, planning for and resolving problems. The characteristics of an effective project Manager are:

- Background and experience consistent with the needs of the project.
- Leadership and strategic expertise in order to maintain an understanding of the overall project and its environment while at the same time working on details of project.
- Technical expertise in the area of the project in order to make sound technical decisions.
- Interpersonal competence and the people skills to take upon such roles as Project champion, motivator, communicator, facilitator and politician.
- Proven managerial ability in terms of a track record of getting things done.

Those involved in monitoring and evaluation of projects should check to ensure that the project did indeed have a project manager with these characteristics or that the assistant project managers actually exhibit these characteristics. There are many projects which fail simply because a wrong person was chosen to lead the project.

Of the above listed characteristics of a successful project manager, which one in your opinion is the most important?

1.6 Project Processes

More often than not, monitoring and evaluation of projects require a careful review of the project management practices. One way to fulfill this requirement is to assess the project process by process to ensure that all the recommended standard activities are carried out. The Project Management Institute's *PMBOK® Guide* (2013) categorizes the project processes into five process groups-initiation, planning, executing, monitoring and controlling and closure. In each process group, there are a number of standard activities which ought to be performed in order to ensure enhanced PDC. These are presented below:

Initiation Process Group:
- Conducting Project Selection
- Defining project Scope
- Documenting Project Risks, Assumptions and Constraints
- Identifying and Performing Stakeholder Analysis
- Developing Project Charter
- Obtaining Project Charter Approval

Planning Process Group:
- Defining and Recording Requirements, Constraints and Assumptions
- Identifying Project Team and Defining Roles and Responsibilities
- Creating the WBS
- Developing change Management Plan
- Identifying Risks and Define Risk Strategies
- Obtaining Plan Approval
- Conducting Kick-off Meeting

Executing Process Group:
- Executing Tasks Defined in Project Plan
- Ensuring Common Understanding and Set Expectations
- Implementing the Procurement of Project Resources
- Managing Resource Allocation
- Implementing Quality Management Plan
- Implementing Approved Changes
- Implementing Approved Actions and Workarounds
- Improving Team Performance

Monitoring & Controlling Process Group:
- Measuring Project Performance
- Verifying and Manage Changes to the Project
- Ensuring Project Deliverables Conform to Quality Standards

9

- Monitoring all Risks

Closing Process Group:
- Obtaining Final Acceptance for the Project
- Obtaining Financial, Legal and Administrative Closure
- Releasing Project Resources, Evaluation of Staff
- Identifying, Documenting and Communicating Lessons Learned
- Creating and Distributing Final Project Report
- Archiving and Retaining Project Records
- Measuring Customer Satisfaction

In monitoring and evaluation of the project management practices, one can simply use this list to check whether the activities have been performed and whether there is enough documentation to support their performance.

Another way of reviewing project management practices is by using the "subject" or "knowledge area" approach. According to ISO 21500, the discipline of Project Management is divided into ten subjects. The *PMBOK® Guide* (2013) refers to these "subjects" as knowledge areas. Each subject or knowledge area has its own processes which for purposes of monitoring and evaluation can form a checklist to confirm the project management practices. The table below presents these subjects/knowledge areas together with the attendant processes:

Subject/Knowledge Area	ISO 21500 Processes	PMBOK® Guide Processes
Integration Management	Develop Project Charter	Develop Project Charter
	Develop Project Plans	Develop Project Plan
	Direct Project Work	Direct & Manage Project Work
	Control Project Work	Monitor & Control Project Work
	Control Changes	Perform Integrated Change Control
	Close Project Phase or Project	Close Project or Phase
	Collect Lessons Learned	
Stakeholder Management	Identify Stakeholders	Identify Stakeholders
		Plan Stakeholder Management
	Manage Stakeholders	Manage Stakeholder Engagement
		Control Stakeholder Engagement
Scope Management	Define Scope	Plan Scope Management
		Collect Requirements
		Define Scope
	Create WBS	Create WBS
	Define Activities	
	Control Scope	Validate Scope
		Control Scope
(Human) Resource Management	Establish Project Team	Plan Human Resource Management
		Acquire Project Team
	Estimate Resources	
	Define Project organization	
	Develop Project Team	Develop Project Team
	Control Resources	Manage Project Team
	Manage Project Team	
Time Management		Plan Schedule Management
		Define Activities
	Sequence Activities	Sequence Activities
		Estimate Activity Resources
	Estimate Activity Durations	Estimate Activity Durations
	Develop Schedule	Develop Schedule
	Control Schedule	Control Schedule
Cost Management		Plan Cost Management
	Estimate Costs	Estimate Costs
	Develop Budget	Determine Budget
	Control Costs	Control Costs
Quality Management	Plan Quality	Plan Quality Management
	Perform Quality Assurance	Perform Quality Assurance
	Perform Quality Control	Control Quality
Communication Management	Plan Communications	Plan Communications Management
	Distribute Information	
	Manage Communications	Manage Communications
		Control Communications
Risk Management		Plan Risk Management
	Identify Risks	Identify Risks
	Assess Risks	Perform Qualitative Risk Analysis
		Perform Quantitative Risk Analysis
	Treat Risks	Plan Risk Responses
	Control Risks	Monitor & Control Risks

Procurement Management	Plan Procurements	Plan Procurement Management
	Select Suppliers	Conduct Procurements
	Administer Contracts	Control Procurements
		Close Procurements

Table 1.3: ISO 21500 and PMBOK® Guide Processes

From this table, it can be seen that the PMBOK® *Guide* has more processes compared to ISO 21500. Whereas this does not mean that PMBOK® *Guide* is superior to ISO 21500, monitoring and evaluating project practices based on the PMBOK® *Guide* processes ensures that all aspects of project management are considered. For those involved in monitoring and evaluation of construction projects, the *Construction Extension to the PMBOK® Guide (2007)* defines four more knowledge areas as shown below:

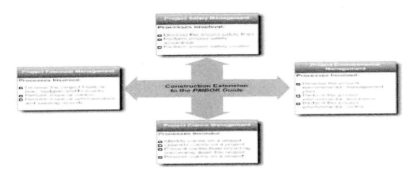

Figure 1.2: More Knowledge Areas for Construction Projects

A checklist based on these extended "subjects" can be developed and used to monitor and evaluate construction projects practices in addition to the one based on the ten generic "subjects." It is possible that one can use other frameworks such as PRINCE2® or any other acceptable methodology to develop a checklist upon which project management practices can be monitored and evaluated.

1.7 Summary

We have now come to the end of this lecture. In this lecture, we explored the various definitions of what a project is and presented the characteristics and key success factors that are important for monitoring and evaluation. We have also discussed the main processes involved in project management and their relevance to project monitoring and evaluation.

1.8 Self-test

Think of an ongoing or completed project at your host institution. Trace the processes that were or have been involved in that project. What are the main measures of success for that project?

1.9 References and suggestions for further reading

Anton, Z., & Romert, S. (2012). *ISO 21500 Guidance on Project Management: A Pocket Guide.* Van Harren Publishing, NL.

AXELOS Ltd.-OGC. (2009). *Managing Successful Projects with PRINCE2™.* The Stationery Office, UK.

Boddy, D. & Buchanan, D.A. (1992). *Take the Lead.* Prentice Hall, London.

BS 4335 (1987). *Glossary of Terms used in Project Network Techniques.* British Standards Institute.

Buchanan, D.A. &Boddy, D. (1992). *The Expertise of the Change Agent: Public Performance and Backstage Activity.* Prentice Hall, London.

Cleland, I. D. & Ireland, R. L., (2002), *Project Management, Strategic Design and Implementation* (4th Edition). McGraw Hill

De Wit, A. (1988). *Measurement of Project success. Project Management Journal, 6(3), 164-170.*

Freeman, M., & Beale, P. (1992). *Measuring project success. Project Management Journal, 23(1), 8-18.*

Harrison, F.L. (1992). *Advanced Project Management: A structured Approach* (3rd Ed.). Gower, Aldershot.

Jiang, J.J., Chen, E., & Klein, G. (2002). *The importance of building foundation for user involvement in information systems projects. Project Management Journal, 33(1), 20-26.*

Jugdev, K., & Muller, R. (2005). *A retrospective look at our evolving understanding of project success. Project Management Journal, 36(4), 19-31*

Jugdev, K., Thomas, J., &Delisle, C.L. (2001). *Rethinking Project Management: Old truths and new insights. Project Management Journal, 7(1), 36-43.*

Kerzner, H. (2008), *Project Management-A Systems Approach to Planning, Scheduling, and Controlling,* 10th Edition, John Wiley & Sons Inc.

Lim, C. S., & Mohamed, M.Z. (1999). *Criteria of project success: An exploratory re-examination. International Journal of Project Management, 17(4), 243-248.*

Nigel, S., et al. (1998). *Operations Management* (2nd Ed.). Financial Times, London.

Pinto, J.K., &Rouhiainen, P. (2001). *Building customer-based project organizations.* New York, NY: Wiley.

Pinto, J.K., &Slevin, D.P. (1988). *Project success: Definitions and measurement techniques. Project Management Journal, 19(1), 67-75*

Project Management Institute, (2013), *A Guide to the Project Management Body of Knowledge* (5th ed.). Newton Square, PA: Author

Project Management Institute, (2007), *Construction Extension to the PMBOK® Guide Third Edition* (2nd ed.). Newton Square, PA: Author

Shenhar, A.J., &Dvir, D. (2007). *Project management research-The challenge and opportunity. Project Management Journal, 38(2), 93-99.*

Shenhar, A.J., Dvir, D., Levy, O., &Maltz, A.C. (2001). *Project success: A multidimensional strategic concept. Long Range Planning, 34(6), 699-725.*

Turner, J.R. (2007). *Project Success and Strategy. In J.R. Turner & S.J. Simister (Eds.), Gower Handbook of Project Management* (3rd Edition). Aldershot, UK: Gower

Turner, J.R., Huemann, M., Anbari, F.T., &Bredillet, C.N. (2010). *Perspectives on Projects.* London, U.K

LECTURE TWO: INTRODUCTION TO PROJECT MONITORING AND EVALUATION

Lecture Outline

2.1 Introduction
2.2 Lecture Objectives
2.3 Distinction between monitoring and evaluation
2.4 The need for project monitoring
2.5 The need for project evaluation
2.6 Qualities of good monitoring and evaluation practices
2.7 Types of monitoring
2.8 Types of evaluation
2.9 Monitoring and evaluation as a system
2.10 Summary
2.11 Self-test
2.12 References and suggestions for further reading

2.1 Introduction

We have deliberately referred to monitoring and evaluation in the previous lecture without any formal definition of either term. This lecture is meant to introduce you to the twin concepts of monitoring and evaluation by distinguishing them and showing how they are interrelated in practice.

2.2 Lecture Objectives

1. Distinguish between project monitoring and evaluation

2. Define the need for Project monitoring and evaluation

3. Describe the various types and levels of monitoring

4. Describe the various types and levels of evaluation

5. Explain why we use the terms monitoring and evaluation together

6. List the qualities of good monitoring and evaluation

7. Understand monitoring &evaluation as a system

Evaluation Definition...

2.3 Distinction between Project Monitoring and Evaluation

Project monitoring is not the same as project evaluation even though they are used interchangeably in practice. The main reason why they are used together is probably because they use the same tools and techniques. According to the Organization for Economic Co-operation and Development, OECD (2002a),Monitoring is a continuous function that uses the systematic collection of data on specified indicators to provide management and the main stakeholders of an ongoing development intervention or project with indications of the extent of progress in the use of allocated resources and achievement of objectives.

Evaluation on the other hand is the systematic and objective assessment of an ongoing or completed project, program, or policy (including its design, implementation and results) with the aim of determining its relevance and achievement of objectives, efficiency, effectiveness, impact and sustainability (OECD, 2002a). We will define these terms later in this chapter. The table below presents the main differences between Monitoring and Evaluation as explained by Kusek & Rist (2004):

Monitoring	Evaluation
Clarifies project objectives by linking activities and their resources to objectives and keeping track of the daily activities	Takes the long-range view by clearly analyzing and tracing the theory of change through assessing specific causal contributions of activities to results.
Translates objectives into performance indicators and set targets and routinely collects data on these indicators, comparing actual results with targets	Examines implementation process and explores any unplanned results
Reports progress to managers and alerts them to problems within the framework of existing policies, rules and procedures	Provides lessons, highlights significant accomplishment or project potential, and offers recommendations for improvement while questioning the pertinence of policies, rules and procedures
Works towards targets by stressing the conversion of inputs to outputs. As such, monitoring reports progress	Measures progress and asks whether targets are adequate thereby emphasizing achievement of purpose and recording any lessons learnt, best practices, comparative advantages and disadvantages

Table 2.1: Differences between Monitoring and Evaluation

For one project that we were involved in, this difference was exemplified by the tools and techniques that we used to conduct monitoring and evaluation as shown in the figure below:

16

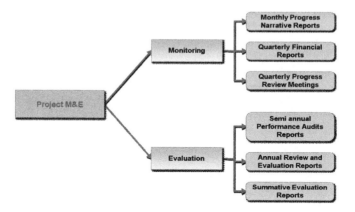

Figure 2.1: Example tools/techniques used in M&E

Based on the explanation we have given so far, what are the complementarities between monitoring and evaluation?

2.4 The Need for Project Monitoring

Project monitoring involves key processes that are performed to ensure that the project delivers the intended objectives. Usually the monitoring activities begin immediately the project gets into execution phase. Monitoring involves tracking, reviewing and reporting the progress to meet the performance objectives defined in the project plan. It allows stakeholders to understand the current state of the project and any forecasts in budget, schedule and scope. Specifically, project monitoring involves:

a) Comparing actual project performance against the project plan

17

b) Assessing performance to determine whether any corrective or preventive actions are required and then recommending those actions as necessary

c) Identifying new risks and analyzing, tracking and monitoring existing project risks to make sure the risks are identified, their status is reported and that appropriate risk response plans are being executed

d) Maintaining an accurate and timely information base concerning the project's product(s)

e) Providing information to support status reporting, progress reporting and forecasting

f) Providing forecasts to update current cost and current schedule information

g) Monitoring implementation of approved changes as they occur

h) Providing appropriate reporting on project progress and status to corporate or program management as the case may be.

Project Monitoring is operationalized through a series of processes as defined in ISO 21500 and *PMBOK® Guide* (2013). It is important that the Monitoring and Evaluation Practitioner understands the activities performed within each process to ensure enhanced PDC. A more detailed discussion of these processes can be found in the ISO 21500 documentation and the *PMBOK® Guide* (2013). Here we present only the sections that are relevant for effective Monitoring and Evaluation of projects:

Process 1: *Perform integrated change control*
This process involves reviewing all change requests, approving changes and managing changes to deliverables, organizational process assets, project documents and the project management plan together with communicating their disposition. It is conducted throughout the project and is the sole responsibility of the project manager. Every project should include a functional change management system to ensure the changes do not upset delivery of project objectives.

Process 2: *Validate scope*
This process involves formalizing acceptance of the completed project deliverables. This involves stakeholders who are brought in to sign off the deliverables as in the case of a construction when architects or construction engineers are called in to verify that a

18

particular level of performance has been achieved before proceeding to the next level. This process brings objectivity to the acceptance process and increases the chance of acceptance of the final product, service or result. Ideally, this process introduces agility to the traditional project management. The scope management plan should contain necessary stages and gates that facilitate this process. Stages are specific periods during which work on the project takes place. During the stages the information is collected and outputs are created. Gates are the decision points which precede every stage. They serve as points to:

- Check that the project is still required and the risks are acceptable
- Confirm its priority relative to other projects
- Agree the plans for the remainder of the project
- Make a go/no go decision regarding continuing the project

Process 3:*Control scope*
This process involves monitoring the status of the project/product scope and managing changes to the scope baseline. This is meant to ensure that that the scope baseline is maintained throughout the project to avoid issues of *scope creep* or *intervention infidelity* (arising from uncontrolled change) are kept at bay. Scope control can be ensured through interim progress reviews and performance audits (to be discussed later). Controlling scope ensures that all requested changes and recommended corrective or preventive actions are processed according to the integrated change control system. It is during this process that actual changes are managed when they occur. Change is inevitable but if left to occur freely on the project then the rate of change could exceed the rate of progress.

Process 4: *Control schedule*
This process involves monitoring the status of the project activities to update project progress and manage changes to the schedule baseline to achieve the plan. This process is concerned with:

- Determining the current status of the project schedule by comparing the total amount of work delivered and accepted against the estimates of work completed
- Conducting retrospective reviews (scheduled reviews to record lessons learned) for correcting processes and improving
- Reprioritizing the remaining work (backlog)
- Determining the rate at which the deliverables are produced, validated and

accepted (velocity) in a given time per iteration (agreed work cycle duration, typically two weeks or one month in case of Agile approach)

- Determining that the project schedule has changed and managing the actual changes as they occur.

Earned Value Management (EVM) technique, discussed in later is used to track schedule performance. Also used in tracking schedule performance are floats/leads/lags and buffer penetration.

Process 5: *Control quality*
This process involves monitoring and recording results of executing the quality activities to assess performance and recommend necessary changes. This is meant to determine the causes of poor process or product quality and recommend or take action to eliminate them. It also involves validating that project deliverables and work meet the requirements specified by key stakeholders necessary for final acceptance. Techniques such as inspection and statistical quality control are largely used in this process.

Process 6: *Control risks*
This is the process of implementing risk response plans, tracking identified risks, monitoring residual risks, identifying new risks and evaluating risk process effectiveness throughout the project. This is done in order to optimize risk responses across the project life cycle. This process is key in determining if:

- Project assumptions are still valid
- Analysis shows an assessed risk has changed or can be retired
- Risk management policies and procedures are being followed
- Contingency reserves for cost or schedule should be modified
  in alignment with current risk assessment

This process uses risk audits to examine and document the effectiveness of risk responses in dealing with identified risks and their root causes as well as the effectiveness of the risk management process.

Process 7: *Control procurements*
This process involves managing procurement relationships, monitoring contract performance and making changes and corrections to contracts as appropriate. This ensures that both the buyers and sellers performance meets procurement requirements according to the terms of the legal agreement. This process is also referred to as contract administration and is meant to ensure that:

- Each party's contractual obligations and legal rights are protected according

Evaluation Success !

to the contract terms.

- Interfaces among the various service providers are properly managed.
- Procurement performance reviews are conducted and documented.
- Claims (also called disputes and appeals) are clearly identified and documented as contested and constructive changes where the buyer and seller cannot agree on compensation for the change, or cannot agree that a change has occurred.

Process 8: *Control stakeholder engagement*

This process involves monitoring overall project stakeholder relationships and adjusting strategies and plans for engaging stakeholders.

2.5 The Need for Project Evaluation

Recall that in the earlier lecture, we argued that a project is said to be successful if it attains operational excellence, keeps strategic focus and exhibits inspired leadership. Project evaluations are conducted to ensure that indeed the project is being or has been delivered successfully. Data collected from project evaluations is used to draw conclusions and make recommendations on strategy, operations and learning (Kusek and Rist, 2004).

Strategy: Questions of whether the project has a justifiable business case and whether it presents a clear theory of change border on strategy. They seek to establish whether the project is relevant given the needs of the stakeholders and whether the project outcomes are translating to the intended benefits. In other words, we are able to answer the questions-are we doing the right thing? Is the project effective and sustainable? To what extent have the objectives been met? Evaluations assess outcomes and answer questions on whether outputs are contributing to achieving the objectives of the intervention. Examples of such questions include:

21

- Is the completed water system what the users' desire and can afford?
- Do the interventions result in real improvements in the health and living conditions in the target communities?

Operations: At operations level, evaluations seek to establish the efficiency and economy with which project inputs are converted into outputs and whether as a result of using the outputs, there is a perceivable change among stakeholders-whether the outputs translate to intended outcomes. Evaluations at this level consider whether resources are being optimized in the production of outputs and whether stakeholders are being satisfied with the project outputs. In effect, the key question being answered at this level is whether we are doing things right.

Questions on economy revolve around mminimizing the cost of resources for an activity ('doing things at a low price'): the economy aspects can include an assessment of whether the procurement process was transparent and provided adequate competition to ensure cost effectiveness; an assessment of whether the financial management processes are transparent and accountable; and an assessment of cost issues like the overall per capita costs for implemented projects, and the unit costs of project components as well as tracking what proportions of funding is used, say, for community level implementation and the proportion that is used for administrative and overhead costs by the implementers.

At this level, we are also concerned with determining whether tasks have been performed with reasonable effort ('doing things the right way'). Evaluations link inputs to outputs and determine whether the inputs (e.g. technical assistance, materials, labour etc) to produce the outputs (such as physical investments; number of people trained) are in the expected number and quality and provided in a cost-effective manner and according to specifications.

Learning: At the learning level, evaluations are concerned with establishing whether there are better ways of doing things-whether there are alternative cost effective ways of combining inputs to generate outputs. Evaluations at this level seek to determine any best practices, lessons learned, comparative advantages and disadvantages that can be included into the organization's repository of process assets to enhance future PDC.

2.6 Qualities of Good Monitoring & Evaluation Practices

Based on the foregoing, it can be concluded that monitoring and evaluation processes are very important for the delivery of any project and must always be designed into the logic of the project before starting off implementation. Without proper monitoring and evaluation, there is no way of identifying any failures as they occur and therefore we cannot implement timely workaround strategies to correct the failures. Like any performance management system, good monitoring and evaluation practices must demonstrate key qualities including:

- Focus on results and follow-up by looking for 'what is going well' and 'what is not progressing' as intended
- Ensure good project design by aligning the project approach to the needs of the stakeholders, ensuring accurate assumptions about the project are properly identified and documented and ensuring that an appropriate organization is used to deliver the project.

23

- Ensure broad participation of key stakeholders in the processes of verifying and validating the project products. This is necessary to ensure broad commitment, ownership, feedback, follow-up and sustainability

- Use a properly developed and pretest results framework with clearly identified indicators

- Focus on results, processes and activities, not people. In other words, do not turn monitoring and evaluation into a witch-hunting exercise.

- Whereas monitoring should be regular and continuous, evaluations should be designed at specific points such as at milestone points within the project. This is necessary in order to control the high costs associated with evaluations.

- Ensure learning through continued generation of lessons learned, best practices, comparative advantages and disadvantages.

- Ultimately, evaluations should represent value for money.

UNDP's Evaluation Office (2002) refers to these qualities as "Good Principles" or "Minimum Standards."

2.7Types of Monitoring
According to Kusek & Rist (2004), project monitoring can be categorized as follows:

- Activity based monitoring- This focuses on the activity. Activity Based Monitoring seeks to ascertain that the activities are being implemented on schedule and within budget. The main short coming of this type of monitoring is that activities are not aligned to the outcomes. This makes it difficult to understand how the implementation of these activities results in improved performance.

- Results Based Monitoring-This looks at the overall goal/impact of the project and its impacts on society. It is broad based monitoring and aligns activities, processes, inputs and outputs to outcomes and benefits. Ideally, all monitoring should be results based.

24

- Implementation monitoring-This is concerned with tracking the means and strategies used in project implementation. It involves ensuring that the right inputs and activities are used to generate outputs and that the work plans are being complied with in order to achieve a given outcome.

2.8 Types of Evaluation

Evaluations can be classified into several types depending on their intended purpose or the project stage. Based on the framework provided by Kusek & Rist (2004), these types are explained below:

- **Performance logic chain evaluation**-used to determine the strength and logic of the causal model behind a policy, program or project. This evaluation addresses the plausibility of achieving the desired change based on similar prior efforts. The intention is to avoid failure from a weak design that would have little or no chance of success in achieving the intended outcomes.
- **Pre-implementation Assessment**-Used to assess whether the objectives are well defined, whether the plan is coherent, and whether resource deployment is well structured. It is also called pretesting or feasibility study or ex-ante evaluation.
- **Process implementation evaluation**- Used to determine whether implementation is following the planned schedule. Earned Value systems are largely used here.
- **Rapid Assessment**-This is a multi-method evaluation using a number of data collection methods including key informant interviews, focus group interviews, community interviews, structured direct observations, surveys. It is meant to give an overview of the behavior of a particular phenomenon.
- **Case study evaluation**-Is used when the organization needs in-depth information to understand clearly what happened with a given policy, program or project
- **Impact evaluation**-Is used to find out the changes that occurred and to what they can be attributed. This evaluation tries to determine what portions of the documented impacts are attributable to the project outputs.
- **Meta evaluation**-Is used to determine what we know about a system and with what degree of confidence. Establishes the criteria and procedures for

25

systematically looking across those existing evaluations to summarize trends and to generate confidence or caution in the cross study findings.

- **Formative evaluation (ongoing, concurrent)**: Starts during project development and continues throughout the life of the project. It is intended to provide information to monitor and improve the project. It is done at several points during implementation of a project. A good example of formative evaluation is when a cook tests the soup as it is cooking to check whether the ingredients are forming well. When done during implementation, it is called implementation or process evaluation. The aim of implementation evaluation is to assess whether the project is being conducted as planned.

- **Summative evaluation**-The purpose of summative evaluation is to assess the project's success in reaching its stated goals. It is also called impact evaluation. Summative evaluation takes place after the project has been completed and the time required to transform outcomes into benefits has elapsed. Following the soup example, when the cook serves the soup to the visitors, the visitors will give feedback either as they take the soup or at the end of their meal. The visitors provide a summative evaluation of the soup project.

Monitoring and evaluation can also be classified based on the levels or stages in the project at which they are conducted. This way, we can classify them as:

a) Impact Assessment Level
b) Outcomes Assessment Level, and
c) Project Assessment Level

Impact Level Assessment is concerned with determining the extent to which the project outcomes meet the objectives of the project. Outcomes Assessment Level is meant to show whether the project outputs or results contribute to the achievement of the defined outcomes. Project Level Assessment maps inputs to outputs. Its purpose is to determine how efficient the project is in translating inputs to outputs. Project Assessment is built on performance M&E systems whereas outcome and impact assessment levels are built on effectiveness M&E systems. As such, Project Level Assessment is referred to as Activity Based Monitoring; Outcomes Level Assessment is referred to as Results Based Monitoring whereas Impact level Assessment is referred to as Impact Evaluation.

The figure below illustrates this:

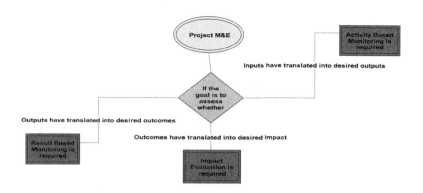

Figure 2.2: Types of Project Assessment

2.9 Monitoring and Evaluation as a System

A monitoring and evaluation system can be defined as a system designed to guide the process of collecting, analyzing and presenting specific data, based on predefined indicators, with the purpose of quantifying achievement (or levels of success) of a defined strategy and guiding future strategy and interventions. We have so far explained that monitoring and evaluation use the same tools and techniques and exhibit a complementary relationship. Monitoring and evaluation practitioners must be able to take a holistic rather than a reductionist approach to projects. Instead of carrying out these two functions disparately, a systems perspective focuses on understanding how these two functions collectively interact to influence and enhance PDC. Monitoring sets the stage for evaluation by ensuring that requisite information is available and evaluation makes recommendations that are meant to improve project monitoring. Monitoring function also ensures that all the recommendations from evaluation are properly implemented. Thus, both monitoring and evaluation function to support each other as organs of a system do.

The system is complete with processes (which we presented earlier in this lecture) and each process utilizes a defined set of inputs which are transformed to outputs using a particular set of tools and techniques. As a system, monitoring and evaluation has a guiding framework within which it operates with clear policies and guidelines governing such aspects as performance measurement, feedback mechanisms and rules on the review of the system. Perhaps it is this systems view that supports the collective use of the phrase "monitoring and evaluation" as opposed to referring to each individually. The complementary relationship between monitoring and evaluation can be likened to the internal and external audit functions within an organization. The internal auditor performs the monitoring function often ensuring that policies, guidelines and standards are adhered to.

The information generated by the internal auditor is used by the external auditor who performs the evaluation function of the organization's accounting system to ensure that it is effective, efficient, economical, relevant and sustainable. Based on such evaluation, the external auditor makes recommendations meant to improve the system and the internal auditor ensures that those recommendations are implemented without disturbing the "equilibrium" of the organization.

In project monitoring and evaluation, we usually emphasize the principles of attribution and contribution. In your opinion, what is the difference between these two principles?

2.10 Summary

We have now come to the end of this lecture. In this lecture, we distinguished between monitoring and evaluation and presented the need for both on projects. We have also explained good practices related to monitoring and evaluation. The lecture also presented the types of monitoring and evaluation and ended with a discussion on monitoring and evaluation as a system.

2.11 Self-test

Imagine that your host institution wishes to conduct summative evaluation for one of their projects. Can you document for them the chronology of steps they will need to go through in planning for this exercise?

2.12 References and suggestions for further reading

Kusek, J. Z. &Rist, R.C. (2004).*Ten Steps to a Result-Based Monitoring and Evaluation System.* IBRD/World Bank, New York, Washington

OECD.(2002a). *Glossary of Key Terms in Evaluation and Results-Based Management.* Paris: OECD/DAC.

Project Management Institute, (2013), *A Guide to the Project Management Body of Knowledge* (5th ed.).Newton Square, PA: Author

UNDP (2002).*Handbook on Monitoring & Evaluating for Results.* New York: UNDP Evaluation office.

LECTURE THREE: MONITORING AND EVALUATION THEORIES, MODELS AND FRAMEWORKS

Lecture Outline

3.1 Introduction

This lecture introduces you to the theoretical framework of monitoring and evaluation by introducing you to the main theories, models and frameworks used in project monitoring and evaluation. These are important because they dictate the environment within which monitoring and evaluation decisions are made. Additionally, understanding monitoring and evaluation theories, models and frameworks enables you to clearly identify the relationships among the various project variables and linkages.

3.2 Lecture Objectives

1. Distinguish theories from models and frameworks

2. Present the main theories of monitoring and evaluation

3. Discuss the main monitoring and evaluation models

4. Explain the frameworks used in monitoring and evaluation

30

3.3 Monitoring and evaluation theories

According to Kneller (1964), a theory can be normative (or prescriptive), meaning a postulation about what ought to be. It provides "goals, norms, and standards" (Dolhenty, 2010). A theory can also be a body of knowledge, which may or may not be associated with particular explanatory models. To theorize is to develop this body of knowledge (Thomas, 2007). Dorin, Demmin and Gabel, (1990) argue that a theory provides a general explanation for observations that are made over time. It attempts to explain and predict behaviour based on observations, and conclusions are based on the data that is systematically collected, analyzed and interpreted. These definitions generally imply that theories are based on conclusions and observations that have stood the test of time and conditions and thus are established beyond all doubt. This notwithstanding, a theory may be modified depending on new observations.

Theories seldom have to be thrown out completely if thoroughly tested but sometimes a theory may be widely accepted for a long time and later disapproved. Kirkpatrick (2001) links the theories of monitoring and evaluation to different learning theories arguing that the goal of evaluation is learning. There are three basic theories of learning namely:

Behaviourism: Behaviorists believe in the stimulus response pattern of condition behavior. According to the behaviorist theory of learning, "a child must perform and receive reinforcements before being able to learn". Behaviorism is based on observable changes in behavior. The responses to stimulus can be observed quantitatively

Cognitivism: The cognitive theory of learning is based on the thought process behind the behavior. Cognitive theorists recognize that much learning involves associations established through continuity and repetition. They also acknowledge the importance of reinforcement, although they stress its role in providing feedback about the correctness of responses over its role as a motivator. However, even while accepting such behaviouristic concepts, cognitive theorists view learning as involving the acquisition or reorganization of the information. (Good and Brophy, 1990)

31

Reinforcement theory: This theory postulates that people are likely to engage in desired behavior if they are rewarded for doing so. The reward is more effective if they immediately follow desired response. Behavior that is not rewarded or punished is less likely to be repeated. M&E helps project managers access information that will enable them reinforce activities that they deem favorable and which will have higher impact on the project results attainment. At the same time the project manager may decide to discontinue some activities based on the monitoring and evaluation results.

Other theories applicable to M&E include:

Systems theory: The theory views a project or program as a system comprising interconnected and mutually dependent subsystems working together to achieve specified objectives. Monitoring and evaluation studies the efficiency, effectiveness and impact brought about by interconnected and mutually dependent subsystems within a project and recommends improvements that will ensure achievement of project objectives and goals

Theory of Change: This theory has been popularized by Carol Weiss in 1995. Carol hypothesizes that a key reason why complex programs are so difficult to evaluate is that the assumptions that inspire them are poorly articulated. Theory of Change explains the process of change by outlining causal linkages in an initiative, i.e., its shorter-term, intermediate, and longer-term outcomes. The identified changes are mapped –as the "outcomes pathway" – showing each outcome in logical relationship to all the others, as well as chronological flow. M&E is concerned with assessing how change occurs within the components of the project and the surrounding environment, which is considered as a result of the interventions from the project. Theory of Change is integrated into the project cycle planning, monitoring and evaluation or applied at different points. These include the pre-planning stages of scoping and strategic analysis, design and planning, and throughout implementation. It can be used to support different project cycle activities, such as implementation decision-making and adaptation; to clarify the drivers, internal and external, around an existing initiative; monitor progress and assess impact of the project.

Explain how monitoring and evaluation can help prove the *Theory of Change* on projects.

3.4 Monitoring and Evaluation Models

Evaluation models refer to approaches or metaphors that different groups of evaluators tend to endorse. They refer to a conception or approach or sometimes even a method of doing evaluation. Usually Models are used in reference to paradigms whereas hypotheses are used in reference to theories. Understanding evaluation metaphors or models leads one to formulate their evaluation theory of how the program causes the intended or observed outcomes. The term theory as used here is not a grand theory in the traditional sense, but rather it is a theory of change or plausible model of how a program is supposed to work. The main paradigms in evaluation are summarized below:

Tyler (1942): Determining the extent to which a program met its stated objectives

Suchman (1967): Evaluating the attainment of a program's goals is still essential, but more critical is to understand the intervening processes that led to those outcomes. An evaluation should thus test a hypothesis such as: *"Activity A will attain objective because it is able to influence process C, which affects the occurrence of this objective".*

Weiss (1972): Development of an approach known as *theory-based evaluation, theory-driven evaluation,* or *program theory evaluation* (PTE) which consists of two basic elements: a theory or model of how the program causes the intended or observed outcomes and an actual evaluation that is at least guided by the model. Popularized the *Theory of Change.*

33

Scriven (1972):

Goal-free evaluation. Examining the stated goals of a project is important but other project outcomes should also be considered. Evaluators should thus cast a wide net in evaluating the results of a program by looking at both the intended and unintended outcomes. Equally, evaluators should not be concerned with reading program brochures, proposals or project descriptions but should actually focus on the actual outcomes. Accordingly, evaluations can be categorized as formative or summative as a way of distinguishing two kinds of roles evaluators play: They can assess the merits of a project while it is still under development, or they can assess the outcomes of an already completed project.

The program model, often called a *logic model*, is typically developed by the evaluator in collaboration with the program developers, either before the evaluation takes place or afterwards. Evaluators then collect evidence to test the validity of the model. PTE does not suggest a methodology for testing the model, although it is often associated with qualitative methodology. Scriven later developed the Consumer oriented model that focuses on the consumer products metaphor.

Stufflebeam (1973):

Context, Input, Process, and *Product* (CIPP) model. Management-oriented or Decision/Accountability oriented model. Evaluation is a process of providing meaningful and useful information for decision alternatives. Describes four kinds of evaluative activities. Context evaluation assesses the problems, needs, and opportunities present in the project's setting. Input evaluation assesses competing strategies and the work plans and budgets. Process evaluation monitors, documents, and assesses program activities. Product evaluation examines the impact of the project on the target audience, the quality and significance of outcomes, and the extent to which the program is sustainable and transferable. The CIPP model asks the following questions:

- What needs to be done?
- How should it be done?
- Is it being done?

34

- Did it succeed?

Accordingly, formative evaluation focuses on decision making and summative evaluation on accountability.

Stake's (1975):
Responsive evaluation. A naturalistic or anthropological model. Conventional approaches were not sufficiently receptive to the needs of the evaluation client. Evaluators must attend to actual program activities rather than intents, respond to the audience's needs for information, and present different value perspectives when reporting on the success and failure of a project.

Evaluators should use whatever data-gathering schemes seem appropriate; but they will likely rely heavily on human observers and judges.

Rather than relying on methodologies of experimental psychology, evaluators draw more from the traditions of anthropology and journalism in carrying out their studies. *Naturalistic evaluation* relies on qualitative methodology but gives evaluators freedom to choose the precise method used to collect, analyze, and interpret their data.

Patton's (1978):
Utilization-focused evaluation. A management oriented model. Evaluation findings are often ignored by decision makers. Relevant decision makers and evaluation report audiences must be clearly identified. Evaluators must work actively with the decision makers to decide upon all other aspects of the evaluation, including such matters as the evaluation questions, research design, data analysis, interpretation, and dissemination.

Guba (1978):
Ethnographic evaluation. Ethnographic evaluators immerse themselves in the program they are studying by taking part in the day-to-day activities of the individuals being studied. Their data-gathering tools include field notes, key informant interviews, case histories, and surveys. Their goal is to produce a rich description of the program and to convey their appraisal of the program to the program stakeholders.

Cronbach (1980):	Emphasized the political context of decision making. Decisions are more likely to be made in a lively political setting by a policy-shaping community. The evaluator should be a teacher, educating the client group throughout the evaluation process by helping them refine their evaluation questions and determine what technical and political actions are best for them. During this educative process, the evaluator is constantly giving feedback to the clients and the final evaluation report is only one more vehicle for communicating with them. The evaluator should not determine the worthiness of a program nor provide recommended courses of action.
Cook (2000):	Program theory evaluators who use qualitative methods cannot establish that the observed program outcomes were caused by the program itself, as causality can only be established through experimental design.
Kirkpatrick's (2001):	*Four- level model.* Well established in the human resource development community, focuses on the evaluation of corporate training programs. Focuses on evaluation of training programs. Proposes four levels that the evaluator must attend to: *reaction, learning, behavior,* and *results. Reaction* refers to the program participants' satisfaction with the program; the typical course evaluation survey measures reaction.

Learning is the extent to which participants change attitudes, improve their knowledge, or increase their skills as a result of attending the program; course exams, tests, or surveys measure this kind of change. *Behavior* refers to the extent to which participants' behavior changes as a result of attending the course; to assess this level, the evaluator must determine whether participants' new knowledge, skills, or attitudes transfer to the job or another situation such as a subsequent course. *Results* focuses on the lasting changes to the organization that occurred as a consequence of the course, such as increased productivity, improved management, or improved quality.

Working in groups, refer to our lecture on the types of monitoring and evaluation. Relate these to the models we have just discussed. State with reasons which model is appropriate for each type of monitoring and evaluation. Also relate each model to the theories we have discussed.

3.5 Monitoring and Evaluation Frameworks

3.5.1 Introduction to M&E Frameworks

We stated in the previous section that monitoring and evaluation models help you identify the evaluation approach or theory on which your conduct of project monitoring and evaluation is anchored. A framework is used to operationalize the model by providing a guide to monitoring and evaluation. A framework explains how the project is supposed to work and lays out its components and the steps needed to achieve the desired results. The framework enhances understanding of the project's goals and objectives, defines the relationships between implementation factors and identifies all elements that could affect the project's success. Monitoring and evaluation frameworks are important because:

a) They enhance understanding and analyzing a project

b) They guide the development of monitoring and evaluation plans

c) They provide a basis for implementation of monitoring and evaluation activities

d) They itemize project goals and measurable objectives

e) They help define the relationships among inputs, activities, outputs, outcomes and impacts

f) They show how activities will lead to desired outputs, outcomes and impacts

g) They clarify the interfaces between project activities and external factors

The goal of the monitoring and evaluation framework is to guide coordinated and efficient collection, analysis, use and provision of information that enable the tracking of the progress made in the achievement of project objectives. The framework assists all stakeholders in:

a) Conceptualizing coordinated monitoring and evaluation system for the project

b) Guiding the development and strengthening of the monitoring and evaluation system

c) Direct gathering of information that will be used in monitoring and evaluating implementation of key project activities

Successfully operationalizing a monitoring and evaluation framework requires:

(i) The establishment of a functional M&E system that provides mechanisms for the timely collection, processing and dissemination of project data that can be used to responsively improve projects and targeting

(ii) That all those involved in the implementation of the project report on outputs of their activities

(iii) That project implementers understand their role in reporting on the indicators and that baseline information is collected where none exists

(iv) Extensive strengthening of subsystems for routine data collection

(v) Mounting capacity building to ensure that the project implementers and stakeholders obtain skills and appreciation of M&E so that they contribute to the availability of data for informed decision making.

3.5.2 Determining the appropriate Framework

There are several types of frameworks depending on the needs of the stakeholders, client or donor, or depending on the typology of the project. Some project sponsors combine aspects of frameworks in a customized approach. Yet others do not include explicit guidance for projects around the selection of a framework. It is important that organizations select the type of framework that best suits their projects' strategies and activities and that responds to institutional requirements. Different kinds of project interventions will need different kinds of frameworks, tools and indicators.

There is no ideal framework and different frameworks are used for different situations. Therefore, a framework that was used for a project to conduct an awareness campaign on the dangers of tobacco use may not be the same as that used for the monitoring and evaluation of the construction of an airport runway. For such a framework to be used to monitor and evaluate the construction project, it would require to be adapted to the needs and the environment of the new project. It is important that before selecting any framework for use, clarify objectives and identify the kind of information that will be useful in reaching those objectives. Also consider what information is readily available. The most commonly used frameworks in monitoring and evaluation are described below:

(i) Conceptual Frameworks

These are diagrams that identify and illustrate relationships among relevant organizational, individual and other environmental or contextual factors that may influence the delivery of a project and the achievement of goals and objectives. Conceptual frameworks help determine the factors which influence the project and outline how each of these factors might relate to and affect the outcomes. Thus, conceptual frameworks explain diagrammatically the build-up of the project results.

A key issue that is addressed by the conceptual framework is the theory of change-the theory of change reflects the underlying process(es) and pathways through which the anticipated change is expected to occur. Such anticipated change may be in terms of knowledge, behavior, attitudes, practices or appearance, at the individual, institutional, community, sectoral, national or other level. Assumptions made in explaining the process of change are usually included in the theory of change so that the limitations of the theory can be inferred early in the process. These assumptions should be stated in such a way that they can be tested and their impact measured and isolated.

Good conceptual frameworks should identify those categories or groups of people who are going to be exposed either directly or indirectly to the project intervention together with identifying the forms of exposure envisaged. The conceptual framework should also state a realistic time frame for which the anticipated behavior change will occur and how this change is to be measured.

(ii) Results Frameworks

Results frameworks illustrate how specific actions are taken to mobilize inputs (financial, human and material resources) so as to produce specific outputs (products, goods and services) and how the use of these outputs leads to short term and medium term change in the conditions of the stakeholders. It also shows how these short term and medium term changes or outcomes lead to actual or intended changes in the society. These actual or intended changes are called benefits or impact. Generally an Output is any of the project's specialist products (whether tangible or intangible), an Outcome is the result of the change derived from using the outputs, a Benefit is the measurable improvement resulting from an outcome that is perceived as an advantage by one or more stakeholders. Where an outcome is perceived as negative by one of stakeholders it is called a Dis-benefit. The manual titled *"Managing Successful Projects with PRINCE2^{TM}* illustrates this relationship using the diagram shown below:

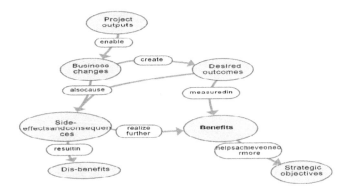

Figure 3.1: Results Framework Relationships

As can be seen in the above diagram, results frameworks show the causal relationship between project objectives and outline how each of the intermediate results/ outputs and

40

outcomes relates to and facilitate the achievement of each objective, and how objectives relate to each other and the ultimate goal. They form the basis for monitoring and evaluation activities at the objective level. Results frameworks are also called strategic frameworks since they are focused on the achievement of strategic objectives.

Take for example a bank's senior staff retrenchment project. The inputs may include retrenchment package, severence pay, etc. The activities to convert these inputs to outputs may include discussion with affected staff, obtaining clearance from labour ministry etc. The inputs and outputs relate to "how' the retrenchment is to be carried out. The outputs of these activities may include retrenchment letters, retrenchment notifications, staff retrenched etc.

The retrenchment will have an effect on the payroll since the staff retrenched are removed from the payroll thus reducing the payroll burden. This reduced payroll burden is one of the outcomes of the retrenchment project. With the reduced payroll burden, the bank may ultimately realize increased return on investment. This increase in the return on investment is one of the benefits or impacts of the retrenchment project. Of course all these hierarchical objectives are quantified and time element allocated to their achievement in the results framework.

The various levels of results framework can be illustrated as shown in the figure below:

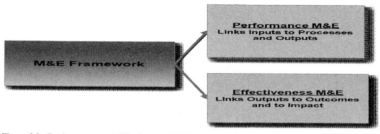

Figure 3.2: Performance and Effectiveness M&E

41

(iii)Logical Frameworks

Logical frameworks or logic models are similar to results frameworks. Logic models are usually presented as diagrams connecting project inputs to processes, outputs, outcome and impact as they relate to a specific problem or situation. They show the causal relationship among inputs, activities, outputs, outcomes and impact against the goals and objectives. Logic models provide a linear, logical interpretation of the relationship between inputs, activities, outputs, outcomes and impacts/benefits with respect to project objectives and goals. Logic Models outline the specific inputs needed to carry out the activities or processes to produce specific outputs which will result in specific outcomes and impacts or benefits. Because of their linear logical interpretation of the project's objective hierarchy, logic models do form the basis for monitoring and evaluation activities across the project's life cycle. They are important tools to guide project planning, execution, communication, monitoring and controlling and overall project strategy.

They show what resources the project will need to accomplish its goals, what the project will do, and what it hopes to achieve. With the logic model, a series of "if-then" relationships can be tested-if resources are available to the project, then project activities can be implemented; if project activities are implemented successfully, then certain outputs and outcomes can be expected; if certain outcomes are realized then certain objectives and goals can be achieved. Unlike the conceptual framework, the logic model does not account for all the factors that may influence a project's operation and results.

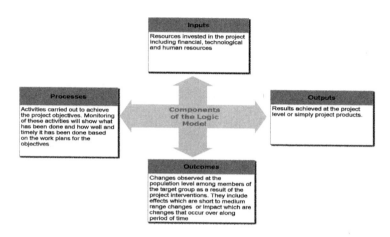

Figure 3.3: Components of the Logic Model

3.5.3 Guiding Principles in the Development of the M & E Framework

Because of the important role served by the M&E framework in enhancing PDC, developing these frameworks must be guided by some key principles. The list of these principles is in no way exhaustive but does provide the building blocks upon which sound frameworks are built. These principles are described below:

Mainstreaming and Integration:	M&E is mainstreamed into all the institution's project interventions. Each project intervention will define routine indicators and reporting formats that will guide tracking the progress made. The framework must fit seamlessly into the policies and programs of the institution without destabilizing its operations. The framework must also flow with the policies of the key stakeholders.
Decentralization:	Analysis and storage of data takes place at the level where it is collected. Simple analytical tools and equipment should be introduced for this purpose where none exists. The key stakeholders are expected to play a pivotal role in this regard.
Simplicity:	The ease with which data are collected, analyzed and reported remains crucial. Procedures can be manual but data

43

collected at grass root level should be capable of being entered into forms and registers. However, data collection should also benefit fully from modern technology to facilitate institutional or program level data aggregation, analysis and report generation.

Action Orientation: Data collected must be used for programmatic and technical decision making. There must be a direct link between data collection, analysis, reporting and decision making at all levels of project interventions. The data will provide information for policy development, project planning and operational management. The system will help to collect and forward only the information necessary for decision making while providing feedback to all levels.

Transparency and Accountability: M&E of project interventions has to be open and participatory for stakeholders and participants at all levels. Those in charge of data collection, analysis, reporting and policy decisions must take ownership of their actions and be able to professionally defend their reports and/or decisions. All stakeholders and participants have to agree on and abide by this key principle.

Refer to the theories and models we have discussed so far. Identify the framework that can appropriately be used to operationalize each of these models and theories.

3.6 Summary

We have now come to the end of this lecture. In this lecture, we distinguished theories from models and frameworks and explained why each is important in project monitoring and evaluation. We have discussed these theories, models and frameworks and determined their appropriateness and linkages.

3.7 Self-test
1. Based on the theories, models and frameworks we have presented in this lecture, which ones do you relate with? Why?
2. You are planning a major training workshop project for all the staff in your host institution. Explain how you will use Kirkpatrick's model to plan for monitoring and evaluation of this project.

3.8 References and suggestions for further reading
AXELOS Ltd. (2009). *Managing Successful Projects with PRINCE2™.*The Stationery Office, UK.
Cook, T.D.(2000). *The false choice between theory-based evaluation and experimentation.*
Cronbach,L.J.(1980).*Toward Reform of Program Evaluation.* San Francisco, CA: Jossey-Bass.
Dolhenty, J. (2010). *"Philosophy of Education and Wittgenstein's Concept of Language-Games".*The Radical Academy. Retrieved 19 November
Dorin, H., Demmin, P.E., & Gabel, D. (1990).*Chemistry: The study of matter* (3rd Ed.). Englewood Cliffs, NJ: Prentice Hall, Inc.
Good, T.L, &Brophy, J.E.(1990). *Educational Psychology: A realistic approach* (4th Ed.). White Plains, NY: Longman.
Guba,E.G.(1978).*Toward a Method of Naturalistic Inquiry in Educational Evaluation,*
Center for the Study of EvaluationMonographSeriesNo.8.Los Angeles: University of California at Los Angeles.
Kirkpatrick, D. L.(2001).*Evaluating Training Programs: The Four Levels,* (2ndEd.).San Francisco, CA: Berrett-Koehler.
Kneller, G. (1964). *Introduction to the Philosophy of Education.* New York: John Wiley & Sons. p. 93.
Miller, N.E., & Dollard, J. (1941).*Social learning and imitation.* New Haven, CT: Yale University Press.
Pajares (2002).*Overview of social cognitive theory and self efficacy.* Retrieved March 30, 2015. http://www.emory.edu/EDUCATION/mfp/eff.html.
Patton,M.Q.(1978).*Utilization-Focused Evaluation.* Beverly Hills, CA:SAGE.
Scriven, M.(1972).*Pros and cons about goal free evaluation. Eval.Comm.,*3(4),1-7.
Stake, R.E.(1975).*Evaluating the Arts in Education: A Responsive Approach.* Columbus, OH: Merrill.
Stufflebeam, D.L.(1973).*An introduction to the PDK book: educational evaluation And decision-making.* In *Educational Evaluation: Theory and Practice,* edited by B.L. Worthern and J. R. Sanders, pp. 128-142.Belmont, CA: Wadsworth.
Suchman, E.(1967).*Evaluative Research: Principles and Practice in Public Service and Social Action Programs.* New York: Russell Sage Foundation.
Thomas, G. 2007). *Education and Theory: Strangers in Paradigms.* Open University Press
Tyler, R.W. (1942).*General statement one valuation.J.Educ.Res.,*35,492-501.
Weiss, C. H.(1972).*Evaluation Research: Methods for Assessing Program Effectiveness.* Englewood Cliffs, NJ: Prentice Hall.
Weiss, C. (1995). *Nothing as Practical as Good Theory: Exploring Theory-Based Evaluation for comprehensive community initiatives for children and families* in "New Approaches to evaluating community initiatives. Aspen Institute, USA.

Evaluation Plan ....

LECTURE FOUR: DEVELOPING A MONITORING AND EVALUATION PLAN

Lecture Outline

4.1 Introduction

4.2 Lecture Objectives

4.3 The need for Monitoring and evaluation plan

4.4 Steps in developing a monitoring and evaluation plan

4.5 Contents of a monitoring and evaluation plan

4.6 Logical Framework Approach

4.7 Summary

4.8 Self-test

4.9 References and suggestions for further reading

4.1 Introduction

The monitoring and evaluation plan is prepared as a subsidiary plan to guide project implementation and to ensure that all the requisite controls are built into the project. The plan is usually developed to reflect the various levels of project performance namely outputs, outcomes and benefits.

4.2 Lecture Objectives

1. Understand the need for and importance of a Monitoring and Evaluation Plan

2. Understand the factors to consider in developing a Monitoring and Evaluation Plan

3. Distinguish the components of a monitoring and evaluation plan

4. Develop indicators to monitor and evaluate the performance of a project

5. Apply the key steps in developing & implementing a Monitoring and Evaluation plan

6. Understand the components of, and develop, a Benefits Realization and Review Plan

7. Create a framework to evaluate a Monitoring and Evaluation Plan

Plan ...

4.3 The need for monitoring and evaluation plan

In practice there are three basic types of organizations involved in project management:

- There are those who HOPE that the project will deliver the required objectives

- There are those who PRAY that the project delivers the required objectives

- There are those who PLAN for the project to deliver the required objectives

Planners usually tend to succeed. It is a basic lesson in management that failing to plan is the equivalent of planning to fail. A Monitoring and Evaluation (M&E) Plan is a guide as to what you should monitor and evaluate, what information you need, and who you are monitoring and evaluating for. Thus, the M&E Plan provides a framework within which project performance will be tracked and reported on. The plan outlines the key evaluation questions and the detailed monitoring questions that provide input to answering the evaluation questions. This allows you to identify the information you need to collect, and how you can collect it.

Depending on the detail of the M&E plan, which in turn depends on the typology of the project, you can identify the people responsible for different tasks, as well as timelines. The plan should be able to be picked up by anyone involved in the project at anytime and be clear as to what is happening in terms of monitoring and evaluation. The significance of the M&E plan is usually expressed using the words of Osborne & Gaebler (1992):

•If you do not (plan to) measure results, you cannot tell success from failure

•If you cannot see success, you cannot reward it

•If you cannot reward success, you are probably rewarding failure

•If you cannot see success, you cannot learn from it

•If you cannot recognize failure, you cannot correct it

•If you can demonstrate results, you can win public support

47

The M&E plan should be done at the planning stage of a project as part of the Project Initiation Documentation (PID) before commencing implementation. This is important to enable you plan ahead of time the data collection activities that you may need to undertake and the intervals at which the data will be collected. You will also be able to determine who needs what reports and with what frequency. We sternly advise against developing a M&E plan during project execution. This advice is based on the well learnt lesson that *"quality is built into a project, quality is not inspected in the project."*

> Explain how developing a monitoring and evaluation plan during implementation may affect Project Delivery Capability (PDC).

4.4 Steps in developing a monitoring and evaluation plan

Developing a monitoring and evaluation plan benefits from the application of several steps as described below:

Step 1: Identify the evaluation audience

The evaluation audience includes the people, organizations or groups that require an evaluation to be conducted. There may be multiple audiences, each with their own requirements. The main evaluation stakeholders include the funding agency, the project sponsor, partner organizations, the project team, regulatory agencies and beneficiaries or users. To these groups, evaluation is undertaken for accountability, learning, sustainability, relevance, effectiveness and efficiency. The number to be included in the evaluation audience depends on the complexity of the project and the evaluation budget.

Step 2: Define the evaluation questions

Identifying the evaluation audience enables you to determine the various information expectations of the various stakeholders. On the basis of these expectations, evaluation questions are developed. Evaluation questions go beyond measurements to ask the higher order questions such as whether the solution is worth it, or whether it could have

48

been achieved in another way. Overall, evaluation questions should be stated in such a way as to lead to further action such as project improvement, project mainstreaming, or project redesign.

Defining evaluation questions also involves identifying whether the evaluation audience has specific timelines by which it requires an evaluation report or information. This will be a major factor in deciding what you can and cannot collect. When developing the outcome-focused evaluation questions, keep them open-ended. Questions such as "*To what extent did...*" are best to evaluate outcomes.

The following framework provides broad types of evaluation questions given specific focus areas:

Process:	How well was the project designed and implemented?
	To what extent did the project meet the overall needs?
Outcome:	Was there any significant change and to what extent was it attributable to the project?
	How valuable are the outcomes to the organization, other stakeholders, and participants?
	What worked and what did not?
Learning:	What were unintended consequences?
	What were emergent properties?
	Was the project cost-effective?
Investment:	Was there another alternative that may have represented a better investment?
	Can the project be scaled up?
What next:	Can the project be replicated elsewhere?
	Is the change self-sustaining or does it require continued intervention?
	Does the project have a theory of change?
Theory of change:	Is the theory of change reflected in the program logic?
	How can the program logic inform the research questions?
	Did the project outputs meet the needs of the target group?
Relevance:	To what extent is the intervention goal in line with the needs and priorities of the institution?
	Has the project approach led to similar results as previous or other Projects at comparable or lesser cost?
Efficiency:	Have the more expensive project approaches led to better results than the less expensive approaches?
	To what extent did the project achieve the intended objectives?
Effectiveness:	To what extent did the project approach encourage the target group to Take part in the project?
	To what extent has the project led to more sustainable behaviors or Change in the target group?
Outcome:	Were there any other unintended positive or negative outcomes from the project?
	To what extent has the project led to the long-term behavior change?
Sustainability:	Can the project continue to generate outputs and outcomes even after the current funding is discontinued?

Table 4.1: Examples of evaluation questions

Suppose you have been asked by your mentor in the host institution to develop a monitoring and evaluation plan for a senior staff training project within the institution. Develop the evaluation and monitoring questions that will guide this plan.

Step 3: Identify the Monitoring Questions

In order to answer evaluation questions, monitoring questions must be developed that will inform what data will be collected through the monitoring process. Monitoring questions are specific in what they ask, compared to evaluation questions since they generate data that is used to answer the evaluation questions. One evaluation question can be fully answered using several monitoring questions. For example, for an evaluation question of "*What worked and what did not?*" You may have several specific questions such as:

- Did the staff rationalization reduce the organizational payroll burden?
- Has the workflow within the organization improved as a result of having leaner staff?

The monitoring questions will be answered through the collection of quantitative and qualitative data. Thinking through evaluation and monitoring questions ensures that data that is collected is useful and relevant and represents the best value for money and time.

Step 4: Identify the indicators and data sources

Once the evaluation and monitoring questions have been identified and the conceptual framework is finalized, the next step is to identify what information you need to answer particularly the monitoring questions (indicators) and where this information will come from (data sources). We consider each of these in detail.

4.4.1 Indicators
(i) What is an indicator?

An Indicator is a sign of progress used to determine whether the project intervention is on its way to achieving its objectives and goal. An indicator is a specific, observable and measurable characteristic that can be used to show changes or progress a project is making toward achieving a specific outcome. There should be at least one indicator for each outcome. The change measured by the indicator should represent progress that the

50

project hopes to make. It should be defined in precise, unambiguous terms that describe clearly and exactly what is being measured. Where practical, the indicator should give a relatively good idea of the data required and the population among whom the indicator is measured.

Indicators do not specify a particular level of achievement, they are neutral and so we cannot use words such as "improved", "increased", or "decreased" when stating an indicator.

An indicator can be described as a quantitative or qualitative factor or variable that provides a simple and reliable means to measure achievement or to reflect the changes connected with a project. This means an indicator is simply a measurement that requires comparison over time in order to assess change. We will see later in this chapter that in the Logical Framework approach, a project is broken down into design elements such as inputs, activities, outputs, outcomes and impacts. Separate indicators for each of these elements (or levels) are used to measure performance. Indicators play the critical role of informing management as to whether a project is being implemented as planned and achieving the desired results as articulated in its logical framework.

(ii) How do we construct indicators?

Construction of indicators is usually done systematically following the process outlined below:
Identify the problem situation you are trying to address. This will be identified as part of the needs assessment to be presented in the next lecture.

a) Develop a vision for how you would like the problem areas to be/look like. May be referred to as the impact indicators. Recall also that as part of needs assessment we talked about identifying the solution's benefits. We must know what will tell show that the vision has been achieved, what measurable signs will prove that the vision has been achieved-for example, if your vision was that the people in your community would be healthy, then you can use health indicators to measure how well you are doing. Such indicators may answer questions such as:
- Has the infant mortality rate gone down?
- Do fewer women die during child-birth?
- Has the HIV/AIDS infection rate been reduced?

If you can answer "yes" to these questions then progress is being made.

b) Develop a process vision for how you want things to be achieved. This will give you process indicators. If, for example, you want success to be achieved through community efforts and participation, then your process vision might include things like community health workers from the community trained and offering a competent service used by all; community organizers clean-up rubbish on a regular basis, and so on.

c) Develop indicators for effectiveness. For example, if you believe that you can increase the secondary school pass rate by upgrading teachers, then you need indicators that show you have been effective in upgrading the teachers e.g. evidence from a survey in the schools, compared with a baseline survey.

d) Develop indicators for your efficiency targets. Here you can set indicators such as: planned workshops are run within the stated timeframe, costs for workshops are kept to a maximum of Ksh. 2500 per participant, no more than 160 hours in total of staff time to be spent on organizing a conference; no complaints about conference organization etc.

With this framework in place, you are in a position to monitor and evaluate efficiency, effectiveness and impact. Development of indicators is a complicated and involving process since the indicators developed will form the performance framework for the project. Always remember the following when constructing indicators:

- Select several indicators for any one outcome
- Make sure the interest of multiple stakeholders are considered. Involve key stakeholders in the selection of the indicators that will be used to measure project performance. This ensures ownership of the indicators
- Know that over time, it is fine (and expected) to add new ones and drop old ones
- Have at least three points of measurement before you consider changing your indicator
- Consider the availability of data for each indicator since some data may be classified and unavailable or may be available only on aggregated levels or already calculated into indicators that may not be the ideal indicators for your project or activities.
- Consider the availability of resources including the cost of collecting appropriate data for indicators, human resources and technical skills.
- Consider the project and external requirements. Imposing indicators from above by those not trained in monitoring and evaluation techniques may be very dangerous for project delivery. Reporting schedules (such as fiscal vs. reporting

year) should be synchronized to reflect different stakeholders' priorities.
- Standardized indicators should be used if available.

(iii) What are the qualities of a good indicator?

Gage and Dunn, (2009) state that when all these factors are considered, we end up with good indicators characterized by:

Validity: accurate measure of a behavior, practice, task that is the expected output or outcome of the intervention

Reliability: consistently measurable over time, in the same way by different observers

Precision: operationally defined in clear terms

Measurability: quantifiable using available tools and methods

Timely: provides a measurement at time intervals relevant and appropriate in terms of program goals and activities

Programmatically important: linked to the program or to achieving the program objectives

Kusek & Rist (2004) describe such indicators as being:

Clear:	Precise and unambiguous
Relevant:	Appropriate to the subject at hand
Economic:	Available at a reasonable cost
Adequate:	Provide a sufficient basis to assess performance
Monitorable:	Amenable to independent validation

Another critical point to consider when constructing indicators is on the question of how many indicators are enough. There is no straight forward answer to this question but have at least one or two indicators per result (ideally, from different sources), have at least one indicator for every core activity, avoid having more than 8-10 indicators per area of significant project focus and use a mix of data collection strategies and sources.

(iv) What are the types of indicators?

Indicators can be classified into different groups or categories as follows:

53

Process Indicators:	Are used to monitor the number and types of activities carried out. Examples include:
	• The number and types of services provided
	• The number of people trained
	• The number and type of materials produced and disseminated
	• The number and percentage of female clients screened
Results Indicators:	Are used to evaluate whether or not the activity achieved the intended objectives or results. Results indicators can be developed at the output, outcome and impact levels
Output indicators:	Illustrate the change related directly to the activities undertaken within the project (e.g. percentage of trainees who completed training on grant writing and whose knowledge improved.)
Outcome indicators:	Relate to change that is demonstrated as a result of the project interventions in the medium-to-longer term (e.g. the number of grants won as a result of the training)
Impact indicators:	Measure the long-term affect of project interventions (e.g. increased return on investment)

4.4.2 Data Sources

Once indicators have been identified and agreed upon by all the key stakeholders, we must set baselines and identify from which sources and using which methods we will obtain the data on each of the indicators. Baselines are derived from outcomes and indicators, the performance baseline is information-qualitative or quantitative that provides data at the beginning of or just prior to the monitoring period. The baseline is used as a starting point or guide by which to monitor future performance. Baseline is the first critical measurement of the indicators. In building baseline information, the following questions should be asked for every indicator:

- What are the sources of data?
- What are the data collection methods?
- Who will collect the data?
- How often will the data be collected?
- What is the cost and difficulty to collect the data?
- Who will analyze the data? Who will report the data?
- Who will use the data?

Examples

Some data collection techniques are described below:

Inspection of administrative records:	**Advantages**	**Disadvantages**
	• Data is already available	• May not contain required information
	• Cheap source of data	• May be incomplete
	• Comparable data	
Questionnaires:	**Advantages**	**Disadvantages**
	• Can collect quantitative data	• Requires respondents to be literate
	• Way of collecting data from a large number of respondents	• Require skills in design, delivery and analysis
	• Systematic way of collecting data from many respondents.	• Time consuming
Focus group Discussions:	**Advantages**	**Disadvantages**
	• Useful way to collect information from groups with low level of literacy	• Respondents may exaggerate or focus on rumors
	• Good way of exploring sensitive subjects	• Respondents from marginalized groups may not feel able to contribute
	• Good way of encouraging community participation.	• Fear of stigma may reduce participation

Interviews:	Advantages	Disadvantages
	• 'Natural' way of gathering information • Good method of 'getting a feel' for a community / situation • Provides an opportunity to see how things are, rather than what people want you to see	• Difficult to make unbiased observations • Can be time-consuming • Can provoke negative reaction from the community if they feel 'spied upon'
Observation in the community:	Advantages	Disadvantages
	• Way of collecting detailed qualitative information. • Good for collecting information about feelings, experiences, perceptions etc.	• Respondents may tell you what they think you want to hear • Recording and analysis of interview information can be difficult • May be hard to check the reliability and validity of information.

We now go back to the steps in developing a Monitoring and Evaluation Plan.

Step 5. Identify who is responsible for data collection and timelines

It is advisable to assign responsibility for the data collection so that everyone is clear of their roles and responsibilities. This also allows new staff to come onto the project and get a sense of who is responsible for what, and what they may have to take on and when. Collection of monitoring data may occur regularly over short intervals, or less regularly, such as half-yearly or annually. Again, assigning timelines limits the excuse of 'not knowing'.

You may also want to note any requirements that are needed to collect the data (staff, budget etc). It is advisable to have some idea of the cost associated with monitoring, as you may have great ideas to collect a lot of information, only to find out that you cannot afford it all. In such a case, you will have to either prioritize or find some money elsewhere.

56

Step 6. Identify who will evaluate the data, how it will be reported, and when

This step is optional but highly recommended, as it will round off the M&E plan as a complete document. Remembering that evaluation is the subjective assessment of a project's worth, it is important to identify who will be making this 'subjective assessment'. In most cases, it will be the project team, but in some cases, you may involve other stakeholders including the target group or participants.

You may also consider outsourcing a particular part of the evaluation to an external or independent party. For an evaluation to be used (and therefore useful) it is important to present the findings in a format that is appropriate to the audience. This may mean a short report, or a memo, or even a poster or newsletter. As such, it is recommended that you consider how you will present your evaluation from the start, so that you can tailor the way to present your findings to the presentation format (such as graphs, tables, text, images).

Here below we present the advantages and disadvantages associated with using either internal or external parties to conduct the project M&E.

Use of in-house personnel in evaluation:

Advantages	Disadvantages
• Familiarity with projects of staff operations • Consistency with management's values • Avoid time-consuming negotiations • Avoid additional expenses	• Objectivity may be questioned • Possibility of organization role conflict • difficulty in releasing from daily assignments

Use of outside experts in evaluation:

Advantages	Disadvantages
• Grater objectivity • Free of organizational bias • Easy asses to division-makers • Time available • Familiar with advanced technology	• May be perceived as 'policeman' and arouse anxiety among in-house • Requires time for contract negotiations, orientation, monitoring • Additional expenses

Use of collaborative effort in evaluation:

Advantages	Disadvantages
• Advantages of both in-house and outside .	• National protocol, practices and priorities
• Experts: plus greater cultural sensitivity	• may constrain study
	• Project participants may not discuss sensitive issues

Step 7. Review the M&E Plan

Once you have completed your M&E plan, highlight data sources that appear frequently. For example, you may be able to develop surveys that fulfill the data collection requirements for many questions. Also consider re-ordering the M&E plan in several ways, for example, by data source, or by data collection timeframe. Finally, go through this checklist. Does your M&E plan:

• Focus on the key evaluation questions and the evaluation audience?
• Capture all that you need to know in order to make a meaningful evaluation of the project?
• Only asks relevant monitoring questions and avoids the collection of unnecessary data?
• Know how data will be analyzed, used and reported?
• Work within your budget and other resources?
• Identify the skills required to conduct the data collection and analysis?

Look up for Kusek & Rist (2004) ten steps to a results-based monitoring and evaluation system. Compare these with the seven steps framework we have used in this lecture.

4.3 Contents of a Monitoring and Evaluation Plan

Monitoring and evaluation plans should be created after the planning phase and before the design phase of a program or intervention. The plan should include information on how the program or intervention will be examined and assessed. Generally, the plan should outline:

a) The underlying assumptions on which the achievement of program goals depend;

b) The anticipated relationships between activities, outputs, and outcomes (the framework);

c) Well-defined conceptual measures and definitions, along with baseline data;

d) The monitoring schedule;

e) A list of data sources to be used;

f) Cost estimates for the monitoring and evaluation activities;

g) A list of the partnerships and collaborations that will help achieve the desired results;

h) A plan for the dissemination and utilization of the information gained.

i) The stated theory of change

j) A monitoring and evaluation framework

k) Evaluation questions and tools

In developing a monitoring and evaluation plan, consider the following factors:

a) Resources: how much money and time will be needed to conduct the activities?

b) Capacity: Does the program/project have internal capacity to carry out the proposed monitoring and evaluation activities, including analysis of data collected, or will outside expertise be needed?

c) Feasibility: Are the proposed activities realistic? Can they be implemented?

d) Timeline: Is the proposed timeline realistic for conducting the proposed activities?

e) Ethics: What are the ethical considerations and challenges involved with implementing the proposed activities, and is there a plan in place for addressing those considerations? Has a protocol been submitted for review by a research ethics committee?

4.4 Logical Framework

4.4.1 The Use of the Logical Framework

Most organizations present their monitoring and evaluation plan following the Logical Framework methodology. The Logical Framework or Log Frame is an analytical tool used to plan, monitor, and evaluate projects. It derives its name from the logical linkages set out by the planner (s) to connect a project's means with its ends. The Logical Framework Analysis (LFA), also known as the Project Framework Approach (PFA) was originally developed by the US department of defense and was quickly adopted by the USAID in 1969. Since then it has been adopted by many multilateral agencies. The Logical framework is a tool to help strengthen grant design, implementation and evaluation; this means that you use it throughout the project cycle. It answers the following questions:

•What is the logic of the overall grant, project, program or policy design?

•How do each of the components of the grant, project or program help to establish an If-Then relation

•Is there a theory behind the change expected or seen? In other words does the change follow the logic proposed?

•Does this theory or logic hold during implementation?

The LFA Summarizes:

• What the project is going to achieve-These are classified as goal or purpose/outcome. A goal is a widespread improvement in the society or a permanent change/benefit as a result of the outcomes of the project. The project outcomes are the intermediate effects of outputs on the stakeholders

• Activities that will be carried out to achieve its outputs and purpose. Activities are tasks performed by personnel so as to transform inputs to outputs

• Resources (inputs) required

• Potential problems that could affect success of project

• Measurement and verification methods for project progress and success

A goal of a project is stated in such a way that not one project can achieve it. It is stated at program level. For instance, a project can have a goal of reducing new HIV infections. There are so many projects that will help achieve this goal, one of them being conducting a behaviour change communications campaign. This project can have several outcomes one of which being safer sexual behaviours. To deliver this outcome, the project will churn out several outputs among them the increased knowledge of, and access to, HIV prevention services. Of course this output will be made possible by several activities, one of which is behaviour change campaigns to educate the public. Inputs to this activity may include condoms, funds and trainers.

This example illustrates the fact that the LFA provides a fullproof relationship that can be used to monitor and evaluate all projects since the relationship is based on a practical project logic. It is a tool to help designers of projects think logically about what the project is trying to achieve (THE PURPOSE), what things the project needs to bring about (THE OUTPUTS) and what needs to be done to produce these outputs (THE ACTIVITIES/TASKS). The purpose of the project is to serve a higher level objective (THE GOAL). As a project design tool, it helps you:

- Organize your thinking
- Relate activities and investment to expected results
- Set performance indicators
- Allocate responsibilities
- Communicate information on the project concisely and unambiguously

4.4.2 The Structure of the Log Frame Matrix
The original Log Frame was a *4 X 4* Matrix-with four rows and four columns. The rows represent the Horizontal logic while the columns represent the vertical logic. The Log Frame is organized as follows:

Objectives	Measurable Indicators	Means of Verification	Important Assumptions
GOAL: *Wider problem the project will help resolve*	*Quantitative ways of measuring or qualitative ways of judging timed achievement of goal*	*Cost-effective methods and sources to quantify or assess success indicators*	(Goal to Super goal) External factors necessary for long run sustainability
PURPOSE: *Immediate impact of the project area or target group*	*Quantitative ways of measuring or qualitative ways of judging timed achievement of purpose*	*Cost-effective methods and sources to quantify or assess success indicators*	(Purpose to Goal) External conditions necessary for project purpose to reach goals
OUTPUTS: *Specific deliverable results required to attain purpose*	*Quantitative ways of measuring or qualitative ways of judging timed production of outputs*	*Cost-effective methods and sources to quantify or assess success indicators*	(Outputs to Purpose) External factors that could restrict outputs from achieving purpose
ACTIVITIES: *Tasks to be done to produce the outputs*	Budget	Timelines	(Activity to Output) External factors that could restrict activities from achieving outputs
	Who is Responsible		

Table 4.2: The Structure of the Log Frame

4.4.3 Steps in developing a Log Frame Matrix

Generally, we follow a three step process in developing the Log Frame Matrix. These are explained below:

Objectives	Measurable Indicators	Means of Verification	Important Assumptions
GOAL: *Wider problem the project will help resolve*	Step 1: Develop Objectives - Top Down • Goal •What issue or problem is the project addressing? • What ultimate objective is the project contributing to?		ssary oility
PURPOSE: *Immediate impact of the project area or target group*	• Purpose •What final results are to be achieved? • Should be clear and brief		ıls
OUTPUTS: *Specific deliverable results required to attain purpose*	• Outputs • What are needed to achieve purpose. Could be several.		) could
ACTIVITIES: *Tasks to be done to produce the outputs*	• Activities/Tasks • Provide a list. May be several for each output • Keep brief and use action words		could

Objectives	Measurable Indicators	Means of Verification	Important Assumptions
GOAL: *Wider problem the project will help resolve*	• Work across identifying indicators for measuring progress • Indicators should define: • Quality - The kind (or nature) of the change • Quantity - Scope (extent) of the change		l) cessary ability
PURPOSE: *Immediate impact of the project area or target group*	• By how much, how many • Timing - By when change should take place		ct als
OUTPUTS: *Specific deliverable results required to attain purpose*	• Two kinds: • Process - extent to which objectives achieved • Impact - monitor achievement and impact of project		se) t could
ACTIVITIES: *Tasks to be done to produce the outputs*	• Indicators can also be: • Direct • Indirect - measured via proxy, alternative		t could m

Step 2: Work Across: Measurable Indicators and Means of Verification

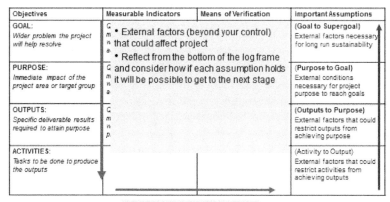

Objectives	Measurable Indicators	Means of Verification	Important Assumptions
GOAL: *Wider problem the project will help resolve*	G m s a	• External factors (beyond your control) that could affect project	(Goal to Supergoal) External factors necessary for long run sustainability
PURPOSE: *Immediate impact of the project area or target group*	G m s a	• Reflect from the bottom of the log frame and consider how if each assumption holds it will be possible to get to the next stage	(Purpose to Goal) External conditions necessary for project purpose to reach goals
OUTPUTS: *Specific deliverable results required to attain purpose*	G m s p		(Outputs to Purpose) External factors that could restrict outputs from achieving purpose
ACTIVITIES: *Tasks to be done to produce the outputs*			(Activity to Output) External factors that could restrict activities from achieving outputs

Step 3: Bottom up - Assumptions

In constructing the Log Frame, remember the following:

- Only a single Goal is defined
- Only a single Purpose is defined-but a purpose can have many outcomes
- Multiple outputs can be defined
- Multiple Activities can be defined. Activities are placed directly under corresponding Output

We do not define OVIs and MOVs for activities. Progress and success of activities are measured at OUTPUT level.

As part of developing the Log Frame, special attention should be given to the formulation of the Project Goals and Objectives. Goals are high-level statements that provide the overall context for what the project is trying to accomplish. A goal is different from a vision statement, which is a higher level statement showing direction and aspiration, but which may never actually be achieved. A goal is the overall broader objective to which the project will contribute.

4.4.4 Example of a Log Frame Matrix: University Academic Staff Capacity Building Project-Grant Writing

	Objectively Verifiable Indicators	Means of Verification	Assumptions
Goal: Improved financial performance of the University	Average annual income from grants accounts for 30% of the total university income starting from 2016.	Annual University's income statements	Faculty members apply for grants through the University
Purpose: To build the capacity of the University faculty members to write winning grant proposals	More successful grants attributed to trained staff than untrained staff starting from May 2015	Grants Register	Faculty members will support this project
Outcome 1: Increased grant portfolio to support research and development at the University			
Outputs:			
1.1 Increased numerical volume of grants under management by the University's Grant Office	Number of grants under the management of the Grant Office increases by 50% every year starting from 2016	Grants Register	Faculty members apply for grants through the University
1.2 Increased monetary value of grants under management by the University's Grant Office	Total monetary value of grants under management of the Grant Office grows by 50% every year starting from 2016	Grants Register, Annual Grant income statements	Faculty members embrace grant writing as a method of increasing University revenue
1.3 Diverse grants under management by the University's Grant Office	Starting from 2016, contribution to the total annual monetary volume of grants under management by the Grants Office reflects the relative size of each faculty/school	List of academic staff and postgraduate students per faculty/school, Grants Register	
1.4 Increased output of supported post-graduate students	Number of supported post-graduate students increases by 10% every year starting from 2016	Register of postgraduate students on university scholarship, Grants Register	

Outcome 2: Growth in the University's research-based academic publications				
Outputs:				
2.1	Increased research based publications by academic staff and post graduate students	• Every academic staff trained on grant writing produces at least one research based publication every year starting from 2016 • Starting from 2016, all Final year PhD. students trained in grant writing publish at least 3 research based articles in refereed journals before graduating	Refereed journals, University research repository, List of trained faculty on grant writing	All trained faculty members embrace research
2.2	Increased submission of research findings in regional conferences	At least 30% of the trained faculty members submit research findings in regional research conferences starting from 2016.	List of trained faculty on grant writing, research conference proceedings, research conference programs and attendance registers, staff reports from chairmen of departments.	All trained faculty members embrace research
2.3	Improved research-based ranking of the University internationally	The University improves in research based international ranking by 5 steps every two years starting from 2016	Web based ranking surveys, University research index	All trained faculty members embrace research
Outcome 3: Increased capacity of faculty members to respond to grant calls				
Outputs:				
3.1	Improved knowledge on grant writing	• At least 40% of each faculty's members trained on grant writing by March 2015 • Number of successful grant proposals increases by 50% every year starting from 2016	Workshop reports, list of workshop participants, Grant Register	The faculty members remain employees of the University for a reasonable amount of time after the training
3.2	Faculty members trained on grant writing	• 950 faculty members trained in grant writing by March 2015 • 19 training workshops conducted by end of March 2015		
3.3	Training manual on grant writing developed	Approved standard grant writing training manual developed during the first month of the project	Training curriculum, physical training manual approved by the University Directorate of training director	
3.4	Faculty members taking up grant writing	Number of faculty members participating in calls for grant proposals increases by 10% every year	Register of applications for training	

Outcome 4: Increased income for faculty members				
Outputs:				
4.1	Successful grants generated by faculty members	Monthly grant income matches faculty's members' monthly salary starting from January 2017	Monthly grant office reports, staff payroll	Increase in faculty members' income from grants does not cannibalize their core teaching mandate
4.2	Faculty members taking up grant writing as income generating activity	At least 50% of faculty members taking up grant writing as an income generating activity starting from 2015	Grants Register, staff reports from chairmen of departments.	
Activities:				

	Activity Description	Required Inputs	Budget	Timescale	Who is Responsible	Prerequisite
A1	Select facilitators	Prequalified list of facilitators	Part of logistics budget[1]	14 days	Directorate of training	Proposal approval
B1	Prepare training curriculum	Training scope statement	Part of logistics budget	3 days	Directorate of training	A1
B2	Develop training content	Training curriculum, training scope statement	Part of facilitation budget[1]	14 days	Selected facilitators	B1
B3	Develop training schedule	Training curriculum	Part logistics budget[1]	1 day	Selected facilitators, Training director	B1
D1	Select participants	Faculty response lists to the call for participants	Part of logistics budget[1]	7 days	Training director	Proposal approval
D2	Package participant materials	List of participants, training curriculum and content	Part of logistics budget[1]	7 days	Training director	D1
D3	Book conference venue	List of participants, training schedule	@ Ksh. 2,800 per day for 950 participants for 5 days=Ksh. 13,300,000 add Training aids @ Ksh. 7,000 per day for 95 days=Ksh. 665,000 Total=Ksh. 13,965,000	7 days	Training director	D1

Activities:

	Activity Description	Required Inputs	Budget	Timescale	Who is Responsible	Prerequisite
D4	Acquire stationery	List of participants	@Ksh. 1,500 for 950 participants =Ksh. 1,425,000	14 days	Training director	D1
E1	Conduct training workshops	Participant training materials, conference facilities and hospitality services, facilitators, training aids, project officer	Facilitation @ Ksh. 2,000 per participant for 950 participants for 4 facilitators =Ksh. 7,600,000	95 Days	Facilitators, Training director	D1, D2, D3, D4
E2	Conduct workshop evaluation	Participant feedback on training curriculum, schedule, content, delivery and conference facilities/hospitality services	Part of logistics budget[1]	19 days	Training director	E1
E3	Conduct workshop review meeting	Participant feedback, facilitator feedback, conference feedback	Part of logistics budget[1]	19 days	Training director	E2
E4	Complete workshop reports	Workshop review meeting feedback	Part of logistics budget[1]	40 days	Training director	E3
F1	Complete quarterly grant performance reports	Grant applications log, successful grants log	Part of logistics budget[1]	40 days	Training director	E4
G1	Compile end of project report	Workshop reports, quarterly grant performance reports	Part of logistics budget[1]	5 days	Training director	E4, F1
	[1]Logistics	15% of (Ksh. 13,965,000+Ksh. 1,425,000+Ksh. 7,600,000) =Ksh. 3,448,500			Training director	
	Total Budgeted Cost& Time		Ksh. 26,438,500	285 days		

Table 4.3: Sample Log Frame

69

4.5 Summary

We have now come to the end of this lecture. In this lecture, we explained the need for a monitoring and evaluation plan on a project. We then discussed the steps involved in constructing a monitoring and evaluation plan and presented the contents of this plan.

4.6 Self-test

Identify an ongoing project in your host institution. Trace the planning for M&E for the selected project and complete a critique to be presented in class. If there was no Log Frame Matrix or if it was not done properly, reconstruct it.

4.7 Suggestions for further reading

European Integration Office (2011).*Guide to the Logical Framework Approach: A key tool for Project Cycle Management*, (2nd Edition). Republic of Serbia Government: Author.

Gage, A.J., & Dunn, M. (2009).*Monitoring & Evaluating Gender-Based Violence Prevention & Mitigation Programs*. USAID, Measure Evaluation. Inter-Agency Working Group, Washington DC.

Görgens, M. &Kusek, J.Z. (2009).*Making Monitoring and Evaluation Systems Work: A Capacity Development Toolkit*. The International Bank for Reconstruction and Development / The World Bank.

Kusek, J. Z. &Rist, R.C. (2004).*Ten Steps to a Result-Based Monitoring and Evaluation System*. IBRD/World Bank, New York, Washington

Osborne, D., & Gaebler, T. (1992). *Reinventing Government*. Boston, Mass.: Addison-Wesley Publishing.

UNDP (2002).*Handbook on Monitoring & Evaluating for Results*. New York: UNDP Evaluation office.

PART II: NEEDS ASSESSMENT, PERFORMANCE AND RISK EVALUATION

LECTURE FIVE: INTRODUCTION TO PROJECT NEEDS ASSESSMENT

Lecture Outline

5.1 Introduction

5.2 Lecture Objectives

5.3 Rationale for conducting project needs assessment

5.4 Needs assessment and baseline studies

5.5 Steps in conducting needs assessment

5.6 Summary

5.7 Self-test

5.8 Suggestions for further reading

5.1 Introduction

Needs assessment is a key application area for monitoring and evaluation since it helps in identifying gaps that require to be addressed through project interventions. Some organizations such as technology companies actually employ Business Analysts who are in charge of needs assessment.

5.2 Lecture Objectives

1. Explain the rationale for needs assessment
2. Distinguish needs assessment from baseline studies
3. Discuss the main steps involved in needs assessment

5.3 Rationale for conducting project needs assessment

Needs assessment involves application of knowledge, skills, tools, techniques and processes to determine problems/gaps in order to identify business needs. With the identified needs, viable solutions for meeting those needs are identified and recommended. Following the identification of viable solutions, needs assessment facilitates the elicitation, documentation and management of stakeholder requirements in order to meet business and project requirements. In effect, needs assessment consists of the business analysis work conducted to analyze a current business problem or opportunity. We conduct needs assessment in order to assess the current environment- both internal and external and current capabilities of an organization in order to determine viable solution choices which if implemented enables the organization to achieve its strategic objectives.

Needs assessment may be requested by a key stakeholder such as a sponsor or donor prior to initiating a program or project. This means that needs assessment work is undertaken before program or project work begins. It is thus carried out pre project. Using the PRINCE2® methodology, the corporate organization or program management, in response to some business reason such as falling sales or decreasing employee morale, gives the mandate to the project executive or board to firstly determine whether there is a real problem or opportunity giving rise to the issue at hand and secondly identify the various options that can be used to address the identified problem or opportunity. The executive or project board then takes this mandate further by analyzing the current situation and making a suitable recommendation in an outline business case to address the situation. This way, the identified solution becomes relevant to the business needs of the organization and ensures that an organization does implement only the projects that maximize their return on investment.

In arriving at the optimal solution, the executive or the project board completes a gap analysis which involves analyzing and comparing the current actual performance of the organization against the expected and desired performance. Notice from this sequence of events that needs assessment and the outline business case provide the key inputs for determining the business objectives and developing the project brief or charter. Recall from your training in project management (and we did emphasize in chapter 1 that there is no way one can be an expert in project monitoring and evaluation without a thorough understanding of the discipline of project management) that the project brief or charter authorizes the initiation of the project by providing the approach to be followed by the project.

We did emphasize in an lecture that one of the key questions addressed by project monitoring and evaluation is that of project relevance. When needs assessment is not carried out, we miss the opportunity to understand the business need in detail and therefore we might pick on a solution that does not address the business problem or that only provides part of the required solution. At times, we may even implement a solution that is irrelevant or unnecessary. Thus, it is emphasized here that needs assessment should be done during the starting up a project process with the intention of developing an outline business case and project brief or charter.

Once a project need is established and formalized in the business case, all the remaining processes in project management are meant to ensure that this business case is maintained throughout the life of the project. Just in case it is established at some point during the implementation of the project that the business case is no longer valid, the project is terminated prematurely and the value of such prematurely terminated project will be the amount of resources that the organization saves by not continuing to implement an irrelevant project.

Think about an organization for which you have worked with. Who in this organization authorizes needs assessment to be carried out? In your opinion, is that the right person to authorize needs assessment? Explain your answer.

5.4 Needs assessment and baseline studies

Many people actually think that needs assessment is the same as baseline studies. This is wrong. Needs assessment is a tool that aids in designing and planning a project. Baseline studies on the other hand are carried out after the project approach has been agreed on and the project logical framework has been completed. Baseline data is used to aid in monitoring and evaluation of the project's progress and thus represent critical reference points for assessing project changes. This is to mean that baseline studies depend on successful completion of needs assessment.

Baseline data is used as a starting point for gauging progress towards the goal and objectives and measuring the level and direction of change. It establishes a basis for comparing the situation before and after an intervention and making inferences as to the effectiveness of the project. The implication here is that baseline data is collected within a timeframe close enough to the project intervention so that meaningful conclusions can be reached regarding changes measured. Another key quality of baseline data is that it should describe the situation and measure factors that the objectives address. Baseline data should accurately reflect the situation for the target population so that its use leads to meaningful inferences about the target population.

Working in groups, list the similarities and differences between needs assessment and baseline studies

5.5 Steps in Conducting Needs Assessment

According to the PMI Practice Guide on *Business Analysis for Practitioners* (2015), project needs assessment is usually conducted following a sequence of steps namely:

Step 1: Identify the Problem or Opportunity
Step 2: Assess the Current State of the Organization
Step 3: Recommend Action to Address the Identified Business Needs
Step 4: Assemble the Business Case

Each of these steps is discussed below:

Step 1: Identify the Problem or Opportunity

In conducting needs assessment, avoid focusing on the solution too soon. Understand the current environment and analyze all the information uncovered. Usually we begin by identifying the stakeholders who are impacted by the area under analysis. Recall from your knowledge of project management that a stakeholder is an individual, group or organization that may affect, be affected by or perceive itself to be affected by a decision, activity or outcome of a program or project. Stakeholders must be identified to represent the three key interests namely:

a) Those representing business interests

b) Those representing user interests

c) Those representing supplier interests

Explain how you can use the PESTLE model to identify stakeholders for needs assessment

Once all the stakeholders are identified, use the Responsibility Assignment Matrix (RAM) to categorize them. A commonly used matrix is the RACI chart:

Responsible: Person or persons performing the needs assignment
Accountable: Person or persons who approves the needs assignment and the business case
Consult: Person or persons to be consulted to understand the problem or opportunity
Inform: Person or persons who will receive the results of the needs assessment

Once the stakeholders have been identified and categorized, the needs analysis should focus on obtaining a deeper understanding of the problem or opportunity in terms of its context. This is done by conducting interviews with stakeholders on the current environmental or contextual issues surrounding the problem or opportunity. The interviews are complimented with document reviews of existing processes, methods and systems that support the business. This can be done through observations by the analyst(s) who may just observe the business performing activities or work in order to understand the current process.

Once the current situation or processes are understood by the analyst, the next step in identifying the problem or opportunity is to gather relevant data so as to assess the magnitude of the situation. We refer to this as sizing up the situation. This is necessary so that we are able to recommend a solution that fits the problem or opportunity. If sizing of the situation is not done, we may end up with solutions that are either too large or too small given the magnitude of the problem. Relevant data can be gathered internally based on the organization's past performance/activities or where this is not possible/available; the analyst can obtain comparative data from comparator organizations or business units. Where no data exists internally and benchmarking is not possible, the analyst can use simulation or prototyping techniques to generate such data. Notice that such techniques require considerable experience on the part of the analyst.

Once the magnitude of the problem or opportunity is understood, the analyst will then draft the situation statement. The situation statement documents the current problem to be solved or the opportunity to be exploited and includes a description of the problem or opportunity, its effect and impact on the business operations. This situation statement will be a key inclusion into the business case (under the "reasons" heading) and project brief or charter and therefore should be done well. For this reason, the situation statement has to be approved by the identified stakeholders to ensure that it represents the situation as is. The approval process can take time particularly where the situation statement has to be revised severally.

Step 2: Assess the Current State of the Organization

This step follows on once the stakeholders have approved the situation statement. The objective of this step is to understand the root causes of the problem or opportunity so that the solution recommended can be seen to be relevant. In this step, we review the current organizational goals and objectives in order to identify the problems that might be preventing or enhancing achievement of these goals. This assessment is done through a review of key business strategy documents and plans in order to understand the industry in which the organization is operating in. The review of these documents is complemented with stakeholder interviews which may serve to clarify any questions arising from the document review.

Following this step, we are able to determine business requirements which represent goals, objectives and higher level needs of the organization that justify undertaking the project. These requirements must be defined before determining a solution since they help in understanding what is critical to the business and why. Goals and objectives are important to needs assessment since they provide the context and direction for any

You are helping your host institution carry out needs assessment for one of their key functions. You realize that the goals and objectives of this key function are not documented. You plan to carry out a SWOT analysis to establish these goals and objectives. Itemize the steps that you will go through in conducting the SWOT analysis and explain their rationale.

change that addresses the business need. All projects should be seen to support the delivery of the stated business goals and objectives. When these goals and objectives are not documented, the analyst may conduct a SWOT (Strengths, Weaknesses, Opportunities and Threats) assessment to establish them.

With the goals and objectives stated, the concern should shift to performing root cause analysis to establish why these goals and objectives are not being achieved or are being surpassed as described by the situation statement. This involves breaking down the problem into its root causes or breaking down the opportunity to understand its contributors. As stated earlier, this is important in order to recommend an appropriate solution. Root cause and opportunity analysis can be carried using a variety of techniques including:

Helicopter Thinking or the Five Whys. This involves stating a problem or opportunity and asking why the problem/opportunity occurs up to a point where the causes become clearer. In an investigation of why sales are dropping, the first level explanation might be due to low quality products. We may then ask why our products are low quality and the response could be because of the low grade technology that we are using. We can then ask why we are using low grade technology. This interrogation will continue until we feel that we have gotten to the root cause of the problem.

Cause-and-Effect Diagrams. These decompose the problem or opportunity into its components. This decomposition helps distinguish the actual causes of the problem/opportunity from its symptoms. Common forms of cause-and-effect diagrams include Fishbone or Ishikawa diagrams, Problem Tree diagrams, Process Flow Diagrams and Interrelationship Diagrams. A Tree Diagram to determine the root causes and effects of the many taxi road accidents for a given transport company is presented below:

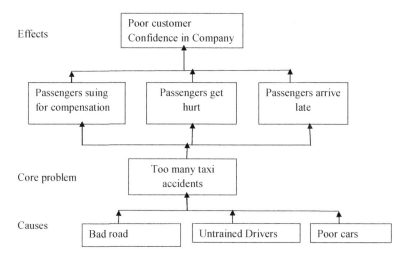

Figure 5.1: Problem Tree Diagram to Identify Causes and Effects

By determining the problem/opportunity and its root causes, the needed capability to address these root causes can be determined. These capabilities can range from simply modifying a process without adding new capability to actual addition of new complicated capability such as a construction or heavy equipment installation. There are various approaches to determining new capabilities. These include:

Use of the Capacity Table. The capacity table lists each problem/opportunity in the first column and lists the root causes of each problem in the next column. The third column then lists the new capability or feature that is required to deal with the identified root cause and thus the problem.

Use of Affinity Diagrams. The affinity diagrams cluster the root causes of a problem in major categories so that common themes can be derived and related problems and opportunities identified. Solutions can then be identified and listed for each common theme.

Competitive Analysis and Benchmarking. This involves analyzing the capabilities of organizations that have experienced similar problems and or opportunities as the current organization. We identify the successful strategies that such organizations have put in place to address those problems/opportunities and explore the possibility of adapting those solutions to the situation of the current organization. Once the capabilities required are identified, we proceed to assess the current capabilities of the organization. This process clearly identifies the capability gaps by checking what exists against what ought to exist. It is possible that following this process, an organization may be found to actually have the required capabilities such that no new capabilities are required. There are several methods that are used to assess the current capabilities of an organization. These include:

- Assessing the processes as they are currently to determine their capability
- Mapping the essential characteristics of the organization to identify the inventory of capabilities. This method is also called enterprise and business architectures method. Business architectures include people, locations, processes, applications, data and technology within the organization. It is important to verify the existence of these enterprise business architectures through a physical check.
- Using capability frameworks. These are collections of an organization's capabilities organized into manageable pieces similar to business architecture. Where this framework exists, it can be used as baseline.

79

Following assessment of existing capabilities, we then compare them with the new capabilities required and identify gaps so that we select the solutions to deal with the missing capabilities.

Step 3: Recommend Action to Address the Identified Business Needs

This is a very important step in assessing organizational needs as it identifies the most viable solution to fill the gap between the current and the needed capabilities. The various approaches to add the new capability are documented together with their feasibility. A ranking of these approaches is done and the preferred approach identified. It is also important to include a description of constraints, assumptions and risks of each approach. This helps in assessing the feasibility and organizational impact of each solution approach so that we can eliminate those approaches that are not feasible. We can then conduct comprehensive cost benefit analysis for the preferred approach.

Feasibility is analyzed based on a set of factors including:

➢ **Operational feasibility**: This assesses how well the proposed solution fits the business need, how the solution fits into the organization and what is likely to be its impact on the organization, how does the proposed solution perform in terms of the non functional requirements such as sustainability, maintainability, supportability and reliability?

➢ **Technology/System feasibility**: This assessment involves whether there exists technology within the organization to support (install and operate) the proposed solution or whether such technology can be obtained cheaply and feasibly.

➢ **Cost-Effectiveness feasibility**: This is a high level assessment of the costs involved in implementing the proposed solution. High level benefits are also identified and compared with costs in a preliminary cost-benefit analysis. Up-front and ongoing costs of the solution are identified so that affordability of the solution is checked against its expected benefits. Also assessed here is the easiness with which funding for the solution can be obtained. Remember that a comprehensive cost benefit analysis is only completed for the most viable option(s) in preparing the business case.

➢ **Time feasibility**: This assessment involves checking whether the proposed solution can be delivered within the organization's time frame and how reasonable the proposed solution's timetable is. We also check whether the solution can be delivered in stages where its delivery timeframe exceeds the organization's timelines. Following this feasibility assessment (which is formalized in a feasibility report), the most viable option or solution is recommended. Given the multiple factors used in assessing a Solution's feasibility, usually we weight each factor and determine a ranking of each solution based on the weighted ranking. The option(s) with the highest weighted score is selected and its cost-benefit-analysis conducted. Notice that cost-benefit-analysis is conducted before recommending a preferred option. A variety of financial techniques are available to aid in this analysis. These techniques are discussed extensively later.

Step 4: Assemble the Business Case

A business case provides the justification for undertaking a given project. It is the reason why a particular solution is implemented. A project must demonstrate the existence of this business case throughout its life cycle to justify continued deployment of resources. We will come back to a detailed discussion of the business case after the following discussion on project choice.

5.6 Summary

We have now come to the end of this lecture. In this lecture, we defined what is meant by project needs assessment and presented the rationale for needs assessment. We then distinguished between needs assessment and baseline studies clearly noting when and why each is done. We have also discussed the steps involved in needs assessment.

5.7 Self-test

To test if you have achieved the objectives for this lecture, attempt the following questions:

1. Explain what is meant by project needs assessment
2. Explain why it is important to carry out needs assessment for a project
3. Discuss the main differences between needs assessment and baseline studies
4. Identify the various roles and responsibilities involved in needs assessment and baseline studies
5. Explain the difference between a business case and a feasibility report

5.8 References and suggestions for further reading

Project Management Institute (2015). *Business Analysis for Practitioners: A Practice Guide.* Newton Square, PA: Author

Rodney, O. (2007). *Feasibility Studies Made Simple.* Martin Books, Pty Ltd.

LECTURE SIX: PROJECT/SOLUTION CHOICE
Lecture Outline

6.1 Introduction

6.2 Lecture Objectives

6.3 Rationale for project/solution choice

    6.3.1 Sacred Cow

    6.3.2 Operating necessity

    6.3.3 Competitive necessity

    6.3.4 Product line

    6.3.5 Product extension

    6.3.6 Comparative analysis

6.4 Characteristics of selection models

6.5 Developing the business case

6.6 Summary

6.7 Self-test

6.8 Suggestions for further reading

6.1 Introduction

Project or solution choice is a very important step in needs assessment as it helps identify the intervention that clearly addresses the gap identified. In other words, it helps bridge the gap between required and existing capabilities within the organization. The solution or project chosen must contribute to the delivery of the organization's mission and vision.

6.2 Lecture Objectives
1. Understand the rationale for project selection
2. Apply the rationale for project selection
3. Develop a business case for a project

6.3 The rationale for project/solution choice

Projects/Solutions are selected based on felt needs within an organization. Project selection is premised on self-defending rationale usually classified as follows:

6.3.1 Sacred Cow Rationale

This is used to enhance the achievement of the overall strategic objectives of the organization, sector, country or program. Such objectives are usually mandatory. They may include the vision and mission of an organization, Millennium Development Goals (MDGs), Kenya's Vision 2030, UN Peace Initiatives etc. This rationale is sometimes referred to as the *Sacred Cow rationale* because such projects are usually pushed from the top management of an organization and are mandatory.

Can you give examples from your context of projects that have been selected based on the Sacred Cow Model?

6.3.2 Operating Necessity Rationale

Using this model, a project is chosen to strengthen a weak link within an organization, sector or country. For example, if a bridge between two major towns is swept away by floods, a project has to be initiated to restore connectivity between these towns. Also, if it turns out married couples are at a higher risk of contracting HIV/AIDS, the health sector will prioritize projects that address this phenomenon. If *Al Shabaab* fighters invade Kenya, Kenya Defense Forces will automatically implement a retaliatory project.

84

Can you give examples from your context of projects that have been selected based on the Operating Necessity Model?

6.3.3 Competitive Necessity Model

This model is used to *"keep with the Jonesses"*. In this case projects are selected basically because competitors are implementing them and in keeping with competition. For example in the banking industry, if Standard Chartered relaxes their banking hours, other banks are likely to follow suit since such a move can easily eat into their profits. If all other banks are relocating their head offices from the city centre to the suburbs, then your bank will likely follow suit.

Can you give examples from your context of projects that have been selected base on the Competitive Necessity Model?

6.3.4 Safeguarding Market Position Rationale

In this case projects are selected to safeguard the industry position of the organization. Organizations that are market leaders and those that are market challengers usually pursue leadership and challengership strategies involving innovation and creative projects. Such projects employ cutting edge technology and are meant to enhance *organizational ambidexterity*-blending efficiency (exploitation of resources to optimize results) and exploration (searching for innovative and creative means of enhancing organizational delivery).

Organizations that are market followers and market nichers will generally select projects that enhance their efficiency in lowering costs. This rationale is referred to as *market position consolidation rationale* and projects in this model can be selected also based on the need to extend the existing product line as in the case of Coca Cola Company's Fanta brand which now has several flavors. In this case, this rationale is also referred to as *product line extension rationale*. The aim however is to consolidate market position.

Can you give examples from your context of projects that have been selected based on:

i.   Market position consolidation rationale
ii.   Product line extension rationale

6.3.5 Comparative Advantage Rationale

This rationale is followed in order to exploit an abundant resource. A project is selected to exploit the abundance of resources available to an organization that are not available to others. For example farmers in swampy areas are more likely to select rice and fish farming projects since they have access to abundant water-logged soil as a comparative advantage.

Can you give examples from your context of projects that have been selected based on the Comparative Advantage Model?

6.4 Characteristics of Project Selection Models

Generally, project selection models are used to justify why a particular project is being selected over the other. It is important to understand that Models do not make decisions-people do. The manager, not the model, bears responsibility for the decision. All models, however sophisticated, are only partial representations of the reality they are meant to reflect. Therefore, no model can yield an optimal decision except within its own, possibly inadequate, framework. When an organization chooses a project selection model the following criteria based on Sounder (1973) are important according to Meredith & Mantel (2003):

86

Realism:	The model should reflect the reality of the manager's decision situation, including the multiple objectives of both the firm and its managers. Without a common measurement system, direct comparison of different projects is impossible.
Capability:	The model should be sophisticated enough to deal with multiple time periods, simulate various situations both internal and external to the project (e.g. strikes, interest rate changes), and optimize the decision.
Flexibility:	The model should give valid results within the range of conditions that the firm might experience. It should have the ability to be easily modified, or to be self-adjusting in response to changes in the firm's environment
Ease of use:	The model should be reasonably convenient, not take a long time to execute, and be easy to use and understand.
Cost:	Data-gathering and modeling costs should be low relative to the costs of the project and must surely be less than the potential benefits of the project.
Ease of computerization:	It must be easy and convenient to gather information in a computer database, and to manipulate data in the model through use of a widely available, standard computer package

The main models used in project selection are summarized below. A more detailed application of these models can be obtained from readings in the discipline of Financial Management and Corporate Finance.

a) Financial Models: These models are based on the cash flows to be derived from the implementation of the project. Commonly used Financial Models are:

Pay Back Period (PBP):	Payback period refers to the duration of time it takes an investment project to recoup the initial investment. It is the duration of time it takes an investment project to return the initial capital outlay invested into it. Payback period is a good proxy for project risk as it enables a project manager to understand when their initial investment will be paid back. *The shorter the payback period, the better the project.*
Return on Investment (ROI):	This technique measures the overall profitability of a project. It shows how much profit an investor earns from every one shilling they invest in the project. It provides a good proxy for the overall project profitability. *The higher the ROI, the better the project.*
Net Present Value (NPV):	Net Present Value refers to the amount by which an investment adds to the wealth of the stakeholders. It is the value of an investment on a time-adjusted basis and after taking care of the initial capital outlay. *We choose a project when it has a positive net present value. We reject otherwise. When a project has a negative net present value, it means that it will reduce the wealth of the stakeholders.*
Internal Rate of Return (IRR):	IRR is the Rate of return that forces NPV to zero. It is a break-even rate of return at which the present value of the cash inflows equals the present value of the cash outflows. *We accept a project when IRR is greater than the project's cost of capital. Otherwise reject.*
Modified Internal Rate of Return (MIRR):	MIRR is the rate of return that equates the terminal value of cash inflows to the present value of costs in a project. *We accept a project when MIRR is greater than the cost of capital*

Profitability Index (PI):	PI refers to the index of the present value of the cash inflows expressed as percentage of the cash outflows. *Accept a project when profitability index is greater than 1.*

b) Economic Models

Economic models are usually based on the evaluation of the economic benefits and costs from a given project. These models include:

Cost-to-Benefit Ratio (CBR):	CBR is a ratio that relates benefits from a project to its costs. The benefits and costs can be expressed in monetary value to give a solid measure. The technique that derives the CBR is called Cost/Benefit Analysis. We choose a project when its benefits outweigh its costs
Linear Programming (LP):	Linear Programming is used to choose projects based on some constraints such as resources availability. We can use LP model when rationing capital to various projects and particularly when such rationing could be for a longer period. This model is useful where fractions of projects can be implemented as opposed to where a project has to be implemented as a whole unit.
Integer Programming (IP):	Integer Programming is used in situations where there are resource constraints but fractions of projects cannot be accepted but instead projects must be implemented wholly.
Unweighted 0-1 Factor Model:	A set of relevant factors is selected by management and then usually listed in a preprinted form. One or more raters score the project on each factor, depending on whether or not it qualifies for an individual criterion.
Weighted Factor Scoring Model:	When numeric weights reflecting the relative importance of each individual factor are added, we have a weighted factor-scoring model. The weights may be generated by any technique that is acceptable to the organization's policy makers. There are several techniques available to generate such numbers, but the most effective and most widely used is the Delphi technique.

Of the project selection models discussed so far, which category do you think leads to a robust decision? Give reasons to support your choice.

6.5 The Project Business Case

Recall that our last step in Needs Assessment was the assembling of the business case. The Business Case establishes mechanisms which the organization(s) can use to judge whether the project or solution is (and remains) desirable, viable and achievable as a means to support decision-making in its (continued) investment. The business case is the reason for running the Project and this reason must remain valid throughout the life of the project.

Since it documents the justification for undertaking the solution by comparing benefits, costs and risks, the business case is useful in gaining initial funding for the project. Most organizations have standard formats of the business case but it should be recognized that a good business case should include a benefits realization plan-a plan showing how benefits will be defined, tracked and managed and also showing who will be responsible.

Once the situation statement is completed, the corporate of program management could pass it on to the executive in form of a project mandate. Recall from your training in project management that the project mandate is the trigger for the project. The executive will lead the refinement of this mandate to develop the Project Brief (which depending on the depth of its contents can be called a Project Charter).

The Project Brief contains an outline business case which includes the situation statement, the proposed solution and its preliminary feasibility analysis. Generally, the project brief is statement that describes the purpose, cost, time and performance requirements, and constraints for a proposed project. Sections of the project brief include Project Definition, Outline Business Case, Project Product Description, Project

90

Approach, Project Management Team Structure, Role Descriptions and any References made say in regard to organizational processes assets or enterprise environmental factors.

The executive then leads the development of a detailed business case from the outline business case. This is done following detailed cost benefit analysis and risk assessment of the proposed recommended solution. Once derived, the detailed business case becomes a live document throughout the life of the project and should be reviewed:

- At the end of the Starting up a Project process and at the end of the Initiating a Project process
- As part of any impact assessment by the Project Manager of any new or revised issues or risks
- At the end of each stage or Exception Plan
- During the final stage as part of the benefits review to determine the success of the project outcomes in realizing their benefits

Following the PRINCE2® methodology, as a minimum, the business case should contain the following section headings:

- An executive summary
- Reasons (reflecting the situation statement)
- Business options
- Expected benefits and dis-benefits
- Timeframes
- Costs
- Investment appraisal
- Major risks

Once in place, the business case becomes an integral part of, and a key input in the development of other, Project Initiation Documentation (PID).

Using a sample project business case, review the contents of each section to understand its composition.

6.6 Summary

We have now come to the end of this lecture. In this lecture, we explained the rationale for project/solution selection and presented various models used in selecting a given intervention. We have also explained the various characteristics of a quality project selection model. Finally, we have explained why a business case is important

6.7 Self-test

Besides the business case, what do you think are the other contents of the Project Initiation Documentation?

6.8 Suggestions for further reading

AXELOS Ltd. (2009). *Managing Successful Projects with PRINCE2™*.The Stationery Office, UK.

Meredith, J. R., & Mantel, S. J., (2003), *Project Management, A managerial Approach*, 5th edition, John Wiley

Project Management Institute (2015). *Business Analysis for Practitioners*: A Practice Guide. Newton Square, PA: Author

LECTURES SEVEN, EIGHT AND NINE: GUIDED FIELD WORK AT HOST INSTITUTIONS USING THE OCAT

Introduction

It is now time to put into practice what has been taught in the six lectures. It is assumed that by now the learner has been attached to a host institution. The learner will use a generic tool, namely, the New Partners' Initiatives (NPI) Organizational Capacity Assessment Tool (OCAT) to do needs assessment within the host institution following the steps learned in class. Based on the findings of the assessment, the learner will in consultation with their mentor at the host institution develop a situation statement, a capabilities inventory, an outline business case and a detailed business case. These will be presented in lecture ten.

Objectives

1. Enable the learner apply the knowledge obtained in real life situation

2. Provide a basis for the learner's project at the host institution

---

1. Using the NPI's OCAT, conduct organizational assessment of your host institution to determine their existing capabilities.
2. Engage the key informants at the host institution to determine what their desired capabilities are
3. Identify and document a project solution that addresses their desired capabilities
4. Conduct a feasibility assessment of the recommended project solution clearly identifying the approaches to its delivery and their viability
5. Conduct a comprehensive cost-benefit analysis of the best approach and complete the business case.

LECTURESTEN AND ELEVEN: PRESENTATION OF OCA FINDINGS AND BUSINESS CASES

Introduction

The learners will each be given 30 minutes to present their OCAT findings and the business cases for the identified solutions. The other learners will get an opportunity to critique the presentation in order to improve it. At the end of the presentations, we expect that the learners would have identified the projects they would be working on at the host institutions.

Objectives

1. Afford learners an opportunity to obtain buy-in for their chosen projects from wider stakeholder base

2. Enable learners improve on their presentation skills

---

1. Present before the class your situation statement, capability statement, feasibility report and business case.
2. Obtain feedback from the class on the presentation
3. Revise you business case based on the feedback obtained

LECTURE TWELVE: INTRODUCTION TO PROJECT PERFORMANCE ASSESSMENT

Lecture Outline

12.1 Introduction

12.2 Lecture Objectives

12.3 Rationale for project performance assessment

12.4 Forms of project performance assessment

12.5 Project performance assessments and early warning signs

12.6 Summary

12.7 Self-test

12.8References and suggestions for further reading

12.1 Introduction

Performance assessment is usually the essence project monitoring and evaluation. This lecture brings out the various approaches, tools and techniques used in assessing project performance. Project performance assessment is also helpful in determining early warning signs on projects so that work around strategies and response plans can be put in place to enhance Project Delivery Capability (PDC).

12.2 Lecture Objectives

1. Explain the need for and importance of performance assessments
2. Compare the various approaches to project performance assessment
3. Use various approaches to identify early warning signs in projects

12.3 Rationale for project performance assessment

Project assessments are a key means of identifying early warning signs on projects. These assessments comprise all types of appraisals and examinations of project documents and practices in order to support decisions, learn from experience or ensure that expectations or formal criteria are met. By identifying early warning signs in projects, performance assessments generally help ensure enhanced Project Delivery Capability (PDC). PDC is defined as an organization's capability to deliver projects according to the client's expectations in regards to time, cost, and quality. These assessments are also very useful in tracking and managing risks and ensuring that the project has continued business justification thus contributing to enhanced benefits realization from the project.

Project performance assessment is about ensuring that the project's success criteria is being met. From your study of Project Management, you classified these criteria into three categories, namely:
- Process Success
- Product Success
- Organizational Success
Can you explain what each criteria entails?

12.4 Forms of project performance assessment
Project performance assessments can be done in different forms. These are briefly described below:

Project Reviews:	Project reviews follow some form of governance/institutional/decision making framework. In some regimes these reviews are mandatory. A good example is the UK Gateway Review process. This process provides a practical framework for project, program and portfolio governance. It examines project or program concepts at critical decision points at the front end and during the implementation period. The Gateway Review process is a quality assurance system to check the successful progress of programs or projects at the specified key checking points (gates) before they progress to the next step. Programs or projects are examined by independent professionals using their experience and expertise. Based on this framework, there are five Gateway Review processes namely:

Gateway 0: Strategic assessment (involves development of program mandate and program brief)

Gateway 1: Business justification (involves business case development)

Gateway 2: Delivery strategy (involves development of project delivery strategy or plan)

Gateway 3: Investment decision (involves undertaking competitive procurement of resources)

Gateway 4: Readiness for service (involves designing, building and testing. This could be a pretesting or prototyping phase or even experimenting on a small scale for large and complex projects before full commercialization or rolling out large scale)

Gateway 5: Operations review and benefits realization (involves establishing the service/product/result, closing the project including managing the delivered solution and performance and decommissioning the solution including exiting the contract.

The first three reviews are at the front end but the last two reviews are checked during service implementation. Gateways 0 and 5 can have several gate reviews depending on the typology of the project. The techniques used in project reviews include interviews, document reviews and team's experience.

Project Health Checks:	Project health checks utilize checklists and Key Performance Indicators to carry out a more formal assessment of the project systems. Project health checks can be used to unearth fraudulent activities during the project implementation. It is carried out at set stages or sometimes ad hoc where specific issues need investigation. Health checks can be useful in determining which aspects of the project need reinforcement.
Benchmarking:	Benchmarking is a form of project assessment that involves a systematic comparison or projects based on some set performance criteria. It is typically used to compare project proposals competing for scarce resources to determine which is most likely to succeed or to obtain realistic estimates, learn how other projects or organizations have solved certain

	problems or rank projects after completion. The choice of which projects or organizations to benchmark against will depend on the organization's level of project management maturity. The choice can be from the same industry (Red Ocean Strategy) or from outside the industry (Blue Ocean Strategy).
Project Audits:	Project performance audits are continuous structured assessments of the project to establish Value-for-Money (V-f-M). They differ from the traditional project audits which includes three major tasks:

* Evaluate if the project delivered the expected benefits to all stakeholders. Was the project managed well? Was the customer satisfied?
* Asses what was done wrong and what contributed to successes.
* Identify changes to improve the delivery of future projects.

Post project evaluations:	These assessments are carried out after the project completion. The goal is usually to generate lessons and assess benefits realization. Can also be done as part of resolving some conflicts.

1. Project performance audits are gaining much popularity in mega project management across the world. Why do you think this is the case?
2. Thinking about your own experiences and project contexts, which of these approaches to project performance assessment have you interacted with? What is your experience with that approach?

12.5 Project performance assessments and early warning signs

We have stated that project performance assessments are important in identifying early warning signs (EWS) on projects. According to Nikander (2002), an EWS is an observation, signal, message or some other form of communication that is or can be seen as an expression, indication, proof or sign of the existence of some future or incipient positive or negative issue. It is a signal, an omen or an indication of future developments. Early Warning Signs (EWS) identification systems are meant to facilitate the identification of signs that can be explored to enhance Project Delivery Capability (PDC) and thus its success. It is important to obtain indications as early as possible of some development in the future, usually of a negative nature. Many crises appear on projects without accompanied contingency plans and require sufficiently skilled project management teams to recognize the EWS and react appropriately. EWS usually present themselves as weak signals-imprecise early indications about impactful events.

We have presented some forms of project performance assessment earlier. These are often used on projects to identify early warning signs to project performance. Other approaches that are used to identify EWS in projects include risk assessment, stakeholder analysis, brainstorming, maturity assessments, cause-effect analysis, project analysis, interface analysis, analysis of gut feeling and project surrounding analysis. It is important to note that designing an early warning system into the project helps identify potential problems as it provides a preventive approach to dealing with issues. Corrective actions are usually expensive since most of them are not planned for and their use on projects may lead to project failure. It is our recommendation that every project should have some forms of early warning systems designed into it. The table below summarizes the utility of the various EWS identification approaches:

SOURCE OF EARLY WARNING SIGN	UTILITY-WHAT EWS IS IDENTIFIED?
Risk Assessment	Potential project problems
Earned Value Management	Excessiveness of limits
Project Assessments	Performance Problems
Performance Measurements	Potential performance problems
Stakeholder Analysis	Stakeholders' expectations
Brainstorming	Potential problems
Maturity Assessments	Potential problems
Past Project (reviews) Consultation	Past project problems and chain of causes
Cause/effect Analysis	Potential problems and chain of causes
Gut Feelings	Potential problems and chain of causes
Interface Analysis	Interface issues/potential problems
Project Analysis	Potential problems
Project Surrounding Analysis	Potential problems and chain of causes

Table 12.1: Sources of EWS

Illustration

One of the most potent approaches to identifying early warning signs is the project Performance Audit (PA). We have already distinguished PA from the traditional project audits earlier in this lecture. The PA is recommended for mega projects that are implemented over several years and cost huge sums of money. We used this approach to track performance and identify early warning signs on a 5-year mega project in the Kenyan health sector. The project involved thousands of sub grantees ranging from community based organizations to government ministries. Performance audit was conducted on each sub grantee at least 3 months into receiving project funding. The audit centered on three areas namely Value for Money assessment, Performance Framework and Capacity Assessment. The V-f-M section was further divided into three sections namely payment to people, payment for consumables and payment/services to beneficiaries. The performance framework involved assessing the sub grantee target achievement, compliance with the work plan and an indication of the overall project objectives achievement.

On the basis of this framework, we generated a performance audit tool with specific questions and instructions and deployed a team of performance auditors to selected sub grantees (hereinafter referred to as Project Sub Implementers-PSIs). The performance audited was conducted on each sampled PSI and a performance score was assigned to each based on the average score for each section of the performance audit tool. The overall scores were interpreted as follows:

Colour Code	Overall Score	Implication
Gold	9-10	Targets have been surpassed by a large amount. PSI has capacity and experience to implement at the next level.
Green	7-8.9	PSI is recommended to apply for a second-level grant in the same category as the first grant.
Amber	5-6.9	A number of areas to improve. PSI requires closer supervision
Red	<5	Bad-list and make effort to recover funding

Table 12.2: Criteria for Ranking Overall PSIs Performance

We conducted the performance audit over the life of the project in batches we referred to as audit quarters for a total of 8 quarters. We analyzed the performance as shown in table

12.3. We used the performance audit to identify various triggers that provided early warning signs that specific risks were imminent or had occurred.

Reporting Period	Mean-Variance Score per section descriptor								Capacity Assessment		Total Sample Audited
	Payment to people		Payment for consumables		Payments to beneficiaries		Performance framework				
	Mean	Variance	Mean	Variance	Mean	Variance	Mean	Variance	Mean	Variance	
Q_1	7.32	3.47	8.04	3.94	8.05	3.93	7.52	3.60	Capacity Assessment was previously not scored		328
Q_2	8.74	1.41	8.15	1.49	8.02	2.17	7.65	3.62			313
Q_3	8.59	4.64	8.08	3.42	9.57	6.79	7.53	5.09			229
Q_4	8.71	4.37	8.11	5.03	9.72	4.82	7.51	7.19			230
Q_5	8.53	2.72	7.92	3.78	8.40	2.13	6.84	6.10	7.13	6.00	263
Q_6	7.83	3.89	8.40	4.15	8.78	5.85	6.38	5.72	6.86	4.51	283
Q_7	8.19	4.22	7.56	2.87	8.43	7.34	6.86	4.65	6.41	4.25	183
Q_8	8.16	4.67	7.33	3.28	8.73	5.24	6.75	5.34	6.47	4.08	177
Q_9	8.46	2.84	7.63	2.19	8.81	15.48	7.54	6.03	7.18	3.22	1535
Total Audited											3533
Pooled Mean & Standard Deviation	8.04	5.68	7.83	5.49	8.33	7.33	7.32	6.88	6.94	4.70	
Coefficient of Variation (CV)	70.6%		70.1%		88.0%		94.3%		67.7%		

Table 12.3: Quarterly Component Performance

102

Table 12.4 summarizes these risk triggers/early warning signs.

Risk ID	Risk Description	Risk Trigger/Early Warning Sign	Likelihood of occurrence	Impact on PDC	Exposure	Detection Difficulty	Risk Value	Risk Status
A1	Under-achievement of targets	Achievement less than approved	Medium	High	Medium	High	Medium	Risk has occurred
A2	Over-achievement of targets	Achievement more than approved	Medium	High	Medium	Medium	Medium	Risk has occurred
A3	Noncompliance with work plan	Over-expenditure, unapproved activities	Medium	High	Medium	High	Medium	Risk has occurred
A4	Late submission of reports	Overdue reports	Low	Medium	Medium	Medium	Medium	Risk has occurred
A5	Non documentation	Incomplete or no support documents	Low	High	High	High	Medium	Risk has occurred
A6	Accelerated absorption of funds	Budget exhausted earlier than approved	Low	High	Medium	Low	Low	Risk has occurred
B1	Delayed disbursement of funds	PSI receives funds long after approval	Medium	High	Medium	Medium	Medium	Risk has occurred
B2	Scope creep	Unapproved activities	Low	High	Medium	High	Medium	Risk has occurred
B3	Infrastructural challenges	Poor/bad terrain	High	Medium	Medium	Low	Low	Risk has occurred
B4	PSI officials hostile to PA	Officials evade PA or hide documents	Low	High	Medium	High	Medium	Risk has occurred
C1	Non completion of projects	Stalled projects	Medium	High	Medium	High	Medium	Risk has occurred
C2	Non achievement of objectives	Under-achievement of targets	Medium	High	Medium	High	Medium	Risk has occurred
C3	Inability of PSIs to attract extra funding from other sources	PSIs rely only on project funding	High	High	High	Low	Medium	Risk has occurred

Risk ID	Risk Description	Risk Trigger/Early Warning Sign	Likelihood of occurrence	Impact on PDC	Exposure	Detection Difficulty	Risk Value	Risk Status
C4	Inadequate resources	Stock-outs in supplies e.g. test kits, condoms	Medium	High	Medium	Low	Low	Risk has occurred
D1	Double accounting of Targets	Reports reflect achievements of other funding	Medium	High	Medium	High	Medium	Risk has occurred
D2	Inaccurate reporting	Unsupported reports by source documents	Medium	High	Medium	High	Medium	Risk has occurred
D3	Misappropriation of funds	Funds misdirected	Low	High	Medium	High	Medium	Risk has occurred
D4	Forgery of project documentation	Documents certified as unauthentic	Low	High	Medium	High	Medium	Risk has occurred
D5	Noninvolvement of PSI officials	Signatories to the grant agreement not involved	Low	Medium	Medium	Low	Low	Risk has occurred
D6	Lack of leadership at PSI level	Lack of clear vision and mission	Medium	High	Medium	Low	Low	Risk has occurred
D7	Wrangles among PSI officials	Splinter groups/camps among members	Medium	High	Medium	Medium	Medium	Risk has occurred

Table 12.4: Failure Mode and Effect/Impact Analysis

For each early warning sign identified during the audit quarter, we agreed with the client and other key stakeholders on how it was to be handled going forward. The client then deployed the agreed workaround strategy. This was so helpful as it significantly reduced the number of non performing PSIs in the project (characterized as RED) as shown in the table below:

Audit Quarter	Color Code								Quarter Total
	Gold		Green		Amber		Red		
	No.	%	No.	%	No.	%	No.	%	
Q1	25	7.6	209	63.7	41	12.5	53	16.2	328
Q2	79	25.2	189	60.4	30	9.6	15	4.8	313
Q3	93	40.6	108	47.2	14	6.1	14	6.1	229
Q4	74	32.2	111	48.3	27	11.7	18	7.8	230
Q5	38	14.8	149	58.2	49	19.1	20	7.8	256
Q6	27	9.5	168	59.4	59	20.8	29	10.2	283
Q7	19	10.4	95	52.2	51	28	17	9.3	182
Q8	22	12.4	89	50.3	45	25.4	21	11.9	177
Q9	193	12.6	1,043	67.9	198	12.9	101	6.6	1535
Total	570		2161		514		288		3,533
% of Total Audit Sample	16.1%		61.2%		14.5%		8.2%		

Table 12.5: PSI Overall Quarterly Performance Ranking

On the basis of the overall ranking, we were able to determine the Value of the project that was at Risk (VaR) for each audit quarter. The concept of VaR as borrowed from Corporate Finance literature is used here to mean the maximum amount the project could lose at any one time. This maximum loss was calculated based on the total amount of money that had been disbursed to PSIs ranking RED and AMBER. The inclusion of AMBER PSIs was based on the argument that there was a high possibility they could transition to RED if urgent intervention was not taken. The table below shows the trends in the project VaR:

Audit Quarter	Total Sample	PSIs Ranked Amber	% of PSIs Ranked Amber	PSIs Ranked Red	% of PSIs Ranked Red	Value at Risk (VaR)- Amount of Money Actually Disbursed to Amber and Red PSIs in Ksh.
Q1	328	41	12.50%	53	16.20%	35,697,135
Q2	313	30	9.60%	15	4.80%	14,283,222
Q3	229	14	6.10%	14	6.10%	7,011,436
Q4	230	18	7.80%	27	11.70%	11,899,000
Q5	263	49	18.60%	20	7.60%	13,769,710
Q6	283	59	20.80%	29	10.20%	24,139,052
Q7	183	51	27.90%	17	9.30%	22,784,889
Q8	177	41	23.20%	24	13.60%	12,147,800
Q9	1535	198	12.90%	101	6.60%	99,154,000
Total	3541	518	14.60%	300	8.50%	

Table 12.6: Trends in Number & Proportion of PSIs Ranked Amber or Red

These VaR were always reported to the client so that they could check whether the values represented normal/tolerable loss or required *management by exception*. The performance audit also included another control-that of Rapid Response Reports. Whenever a performance auditor audited a PSI and detected outright fraud, they would complete a Rapid Response Report and send it to the client within the same day to ensure rapid action to protect the project from further fraud or loss.

We also used performance audit on another 5-year pan African project and it proved to be very useful in enhancing PDC. At the end of every audit, we would discuss with the client the various actions to be taken on the grantee and the client would then pursue the implementation of the agreed workaround strategies to optimize project delivery. Notice that project performance audits are continuous structured assessments unlike the traditional audits that are periodic. We now turn to another very useful approach to identifying EWS while determining the actual levels of project performance.

 Project performance assessments are done at various stages of the project such as at project start-up, during early stages and during execution. From your experience and based on your context, can you identify at least three common early warning signs at each stage?

12.6 Summary

We have now come to the end of this lecture. In this lecture, we explained the rationale for project performance assessment and presented the various approaches and techniques used to conduct performance assessment on a project. We also discussed the identification of early warning signs on projects.

12.7 Self-test

Using the Gateway Review Process presented in section 12.4, explain how a project can make the Go/No-Go decisions.

12.8 Suggestions for further reading

Klakegg, O.J., Andersen, B., Williams, T., Walker, D.H.T., & Magnussen, O.M. (2012).*Identifying and acting on early warning signs in Complex Projects. Project Management Journal*, 43(2), 37-53.
Klakegg, O.J., Andersen, B., Williams, T., Walker, D.H.T., & Magnussen, O.M. (2010).*Early Warning Signs in Complex Projects*. Newton Square, PA: Project Management Institute.
Nikander, I.O. (2002). *Early Warning Signs: A phenomenon in project management* (unpublished dissertation for doctor of science in technology).Helsinki University of Technology, Espoo, Finland.
Sara, H-K., Bjorn, A., & Hans, P.K. (2013).*A Review on Possible Approaches for Detecting Early Warning Signs in Projects. Project Management Journal*, 44(5), 55-69.

LECTURE THIRTEEN: VALUE FOR MONEY ASSESSMENT
Lecture Outline

13.1 Introduction

13.2 Lecture Objectives

13.3 Rationale for V-F-M assessment

13.4 Assessing project economy

13.5 Assessing project efficiency

13.6 Assessing project effectiveness

13.7 Summary

13.8 Self-test

13.9 References and suggestions for further reading

13.1 Introduction
Project audits involve a central theme which is establishing whether the project is delivering value to intended beneficiaries given the level of the amount of money committed. Value-for-Money (VfM) assessments help determine whether the project is worth continuing with or whether its approach needs to be redesigned in order to benefit the intended users.

13.2 Lecture Objectives

1. Introduce the learner to the concept of and need for Value-for-Money
2. Provide the learner a structured approach to conducting Value-for-Money assessments

13.3 Rationale for V-F-M assessment

Central to Project Performance Audits is the concept of Value for Money. This generally involves comparison of inputs and outputs to ensure achievement of Value for Money (VFM). VFM is a term used to describe whether or not an organisation has obtained the maximum benefit from the goods and services it both acquires and

109

provides, within the resources available to it. It not only measures the cost of goods and services, it also judges whether they constitute good value for money by taking account of the following variables:

•The mix of quality, cost, resources use e.g. are the specifications followed, are the unit costs acceptable, are the community mobilisation and hygiene education activities carried out cost-effectively etc.

•Fitness for purpose, e.g. does the support delivered satisfy the needs of the communities and provide the desired service level, are the sanitation standards adequate to provide improvements in hygiene etc.

•Timeliness, e.g. are the support activities implemented within the projected time frame, are deliveries of training and capacity building activities integrated effectively in the hardware delivery schedules etc.

Achieving VFM is also often described in terms of the 'three Es' – economy, efficiency and effectiveness. These are explained in the sections that follow.

Remember the "Iron Triangle" used to define the critical dimensions of a project? Explain how Value-for-Money assessments help to operationalize this "triangle"

13.4 Assessing Project Economy

Economy involves minimizing the cost of resources for an activity i.e doing things at a low price. The economy aspects can include an assessment of:

- Whether the procurement process was transparent and provided adequate competition to ensure cost effectiveness;
- Whether the financial management processes are transparent and accountable;
- Cost issues like the overall per capita costs for implemented projects and the unit costs for water supply, sanitation and hygiene, education components
- What proportions of funding is used for community level implementation and the proportion that is used for administrative and overhead costs by the implementers.

Procurement procedures and regulations are a key input in the process of assessing a project's economy.

13.5 Assessing Project Efficiency

Efficiency involves performing tasks with reasonable effort i.e. doing things the right way. VFM studies link inputs to outputs and determine whether the inputs (technical assistance, materials, labour etc) to produce the outputs (physical investments; number of people trained) are in the expected number and quality and provided in a cost-effective manner and according to specifications etc.

13.6 Assessing Project Effectiveness

Effectiveness assessment involves the extent to which objectives are met i.e. doing the right things. VFM Studies assess outcomes by answering the question: are the outputs contributing to achieving the objectives of the intervention e.g.:

- Is the completed water system what the users desire and can afford?
- Do the interventions result in real improvements in the health and living conditions in the target communities?
- Do the interventions result in improved access to health services for example family planning or safe motherhood services?

To be able to effectively draw conclusions on VfM, it is always important to include the beneficiary sentiment in your analysis by collecting data on their levels of satisfaction. Some practitioners also include the Equity as the 4[th]E in assessing VfM. Equity means ensuring that benefits are distributed fairly.

The main methods of evaluating Value-for-Money are:

- Cost Effectiveness Analysis (CE analysis)
- Cost Utility Analysis (CU analysis)
- Cost Benefit Analysis
- Social Return on Investment (SROI)
- Rank correlation of cost versus impact
- Basic Efficiency Resource Analysis (BER analysis)

These methods will be defined in the next lecture and their application will become obvious then.

 Assume that you are conducting audit of a project whose interventions are meant to reduce new HIV infections among the youth in Kenya through behavior change communications campaign. Draw up a checklist of questions that you will use to assess whether the project is delivering VfM.

13.7 Summary

We have now come to the end of this lecture. In this lecture, we explained the concept of and rationale for assessing a project for Value-for-Money. We have also explained the dimensions of Value-for-Money assessment and concluded that the beneficiary is always at the centre of V-f-M studies and must always be involved.

13.8 Self-test

Assume that you have collected performance data regarding the behavior change communication campaign project from the implementing organizations and you now wish to corroborate these data with the beneficiary sentiment. You have identified a key beneficiary whom you want to set up a meeting with. Develop a short skit representing your conversation with the key beneficiary from the time of booking the appointment to the actual interview. This skit should be presented in class in form of a short play.

13.9 Suggestions for further reading

Farida, F. (2013).*Evaluation Methods for Assessing Value for Money*. Better Evaluation.
Levin, H. M. &McEwan, P.J.(2001).*Cost-effectiveness-analysis: Methods and applications*. Sage Publications, California.

LECTURE FOURTEEN: METHODS OF ASSESSING PROJECT VALUE FOR MONEY

Lecture Outline

14.1 Introduction

14.2 Lecture Objectives

14.3 Methods of assessing project value for money

14.4 Issuescommonto all VfM methods

14.5 Summary

14.6 Self-test

14.7 Suggestions for further reading

14.1 Introduction

Value for Money (VfM) is a concern in procurement and implementation of programs worldwide. Determining whether programs or activities provide value for money is of interest to national governments as well as international donors and non-government organizations. In the international domain, the issue of VfM has become a policy imperative. Economic analysis helps in determining the fundamental question of the central government: how to allocate scarce resources among a large number of competing projects.

To determine which programs are worth-while, the government focuses on key questions: is this project worth it, what are the benefits and what are the costs, could the private sector do a better job, is it cost-effective compared with alternatives? The idea of judging the utility of social interventions has gained wide-spread public acceptance.

114

14.2 Lecture Objectives

1. Explain the main techniques used in assessing Value for Money

2. Demonstrate how to use Cost-Effectiveness Analysis in determining a Project's Value for Money

14.3 Methods of assessing Project Value for Money

There are six main methods that can be used to assess VfM. These are:

- Cost Effectiveness Analysis (CE analysis)
- Cost Utility Analysis (CU analysis)
- Cost Benefit Analysis
- Social Return on Investment (SROI)
- Rank correlation of cost versus impact
- Basic Efficiency Resource Analysis (BER analysis)

Different methods are recommended in different situations as shown below:

- If the evaluator wants to compare alternative programs that aim to reach the same goal then the right method is Cost Effectiveness Analysis

- If the evaluator wants to compare alternative programs that aim to reach different goals then the right method to use is Cost Benefit Analysis

- If the evaluator wants to compare alternative programs that occur in different sectors then the right method to use is Cost Benefit Analysis

- If the evaluator wants to understand whether program or project benefits outweigh costs then the right method to use is Cost Benefit Analysis

- If the evaluator wants to consider individual Preferences in determining value for money then the right method is Cost Utility Analysis

- If the evaluator wants to consider social costs in calculating value for money then the right method to use is Social Return On Investment

- If the evaluator wants to compare the impact and performance of each unit relative to other units then the recommended methods are Basic Efficiency Resource Analysis and Rank Correlation

Which of these methods have you interacted with? What is your experience?

These six methods can be categorized in terms of three groups with each group examining the relationship between costs and benefits in a particular way. Table 14.1 summarizes the methods by category.

Working in groups, state the main advantages and disadvantages of each of these methods and identify the expertise required to use each method.

14.4 Issues common to all VfM methods

There are a number of questions an evaluator should ask regardless of which method they choose for assessing VfM:

- How will value be measured? Will it include economy, efficiency, and effectiveness? Will it include equity?
- Who will decide value? Will this be a participatory analysis?
- Is the evaluation assessing the value of one project or comparing a number of projects?
- Will the evaluation measure in monetary terms or will it use a proxy measure of value?
- How will the evaluation process make sure costs and benefits are agreed and transparent?
- Will these methods be used in ways that promote/enable participation and accountability to communities and partners?

	Method	Description	Similarities and differences
Group1	Cost Effectiveness Analysis	CEA involves the evaluation of two or more alternatives, based on the relative costs and outcomes (effects), in reaching a particular goal. This method can be used when comparing programs that aim to achieve the same goal.	The main difference between the two methods is that CUA takes beneficiary perspectives into account. Well-known applications of CU analysis is in the health sector, with the use of Quality Adjusted Life Years (QALYs).The QALY allows each potential program to be measured according to the extent to which it extends life expectancy while also improving the quality of each year lived.
	Cost Utility Analysis	The evaluation of two or more alternatives by comparing their costs to their utility or value (a measure of effectiveness developed from the preferences of individuals).This method can be used where monetizing outcomes is not possible or appropriate. This method is most commonly used in health through quality adjusted life years (QALY).The QALY allows the comparison of medical interventions by the number of years that they extend life.	
Group2	Cost Benefit Analysis	CBA involves the evaluation of alternatives by identifying the costs and benefits of each alternative in money terms, and adjusting for time. This method can be used to identify if a course of action is worthwhile in an absolute sense-whether the costs outweigh the benefits-and allows for comparison among alternatives that do not share the same objective or the same sector.	Cost Benefit Analysis and Social Return on Investment evaluate whether a program is beneficial in an absolute sense. They both monetize outcomes. Both methods allow for comparison of programs with different objectives or from different sectors. The difference between them is that SROI measures social, environmental and economic costs and benefits.
	Social Return on Investment	Measures social, environmental and economic costs and benefits. Like Cost Benefit analysis, SROI can be used when comparing programs with different goals or in different sectors.	
Group3	Rank correlation Of cost versus impact	Allows for the relative measurement of VfM across a portfolio of initiatives.	Both these evaluate the relative costs and benefits of many programs. The first method ranks and correlates costs and impact while the second examines relative value by plotting programs on a four quadrant graph based on costs and impacts.
	Basic Efficiency Resource Analysis	Provides a framework for evaluating complex programs by comparing impact to resources and offering a relative perspective on performance where units analyzed are judged in comparison to other peer units.	

Table 14.1: Methods of assessing Value for Money

118

Illustration

We were recently involved in an operational assessment of some health care project in Kenya. Part of this involved conducting a CEA over the life of the project. The project involved provision of health facilities to hard to reach populations through the use of mobile clinics and the assessment was carried out to establish whether this intervention should be up-scaled or whether health care should continue to be provided using static facilities. Each mobile clinic was tied to a comparator static facility for purposes of conducting CEA.

We categorized the annual costs of running these health facilities into personnel, operating and fixed costs. Personnel costs were aggregated from personnel records at the facilities and the values obtained were counterchecked with key informants at sub county and county levels to ascertain their accuracy and completeness. Maintenance costs were determined as a proportion of the historical cost of the underlying assets. Generally, costs of maintaining buildings, tents, motorcycles and trailers for mobile clinics was calculated as 5% of their historical cost whereas the cost of maintaining furniture and equipment was determined as 2.5% of their historical cost. The annual fixed costs were based on the historical costs of the fixed assets. Fixed costs were determined based on the useful lives of the fixed assets. Using straight line method, depreciation amounts were determined for each asset by dividing historical cost by its projected useful life. These depreciation values formed the fixed annualized costs of running the mobile clinics.

Data on utilization of health care services were obtained from HMIS records and these were counterchecked against the facility data contained in the DHIS for the same period. Since in all cases data from the HMIS significantly differed with that in the DHIS. Data reconciliation was done by calculating the average of the utilization recorded in HMIS and DHIS. We used these averages to calculate the cost effectiveness ratios. Utilization of healthcare services per facility was determined by aggregating the number of

119

clients/patients recorded to have attended/benefited from OPD and MCH/FP services. This was done by averaging data for the period 2011-2014. Cost effectiveness ratios were then calculated by dividing the annual costs into the annual health service utilization. Assuming that choosing a mobile health facility excluded choosing a static facility; we went ahead to determine the Incremental Cost Effectiveness Ratios (ICER). These ratios were calculated by taking incremental costs of choosing a mobile clinic and dividing it into the incremental service utilization for the mobile clinic.

Based on this approach, we calculated the CERs as shown in Table 14.2. The results in Table 14.2indicate that Mobile Clinic 2 (MC2) has the lowest CER despite having the highest annual cost. Thus, it costs Ksh. 454.7 on average to provide healthcare service to each contact/patient/client at MC2. This is followed by MC3 where the results indicate that it costs Ksh. 538.8 to provide healthcare service to each contact/patient/client. Static Clinic 1 (SC1) recorded the highest cost of providing health care service per person at Ksh. 9,263. The general conclusion here is that there is a difference in cost effectiveness between service provision by MCs and SCs and this difference is in favour of MCs.

Analysis of ICER shows that by operating MC1 in place of SC1, the cost per contact drops significantly to Ksh. 208.9 which is lower than the arithmetic mean of the CERs for the two facilities. The explanation here is founded in economies of scope implying that if the current resources used at SC1were to be added to those at MC1, service utilization will significantly increase thus lowering the cost per contact. Again, if MC2 was to be operated in place of SC2 with all the resources at SC2 transferred to MC2, the cost of service provision will drop to Ksh. 220.7 per contact. This is also lower than the arithmetic mean of the per contact costs for the two facilities combined. The scenario is even more interesting if the resources at SC3 were to be transferred to MC3. The indication here is that there will be a reduction in the component costs of providing healthcare at MC3 with an increase in service utilization! It is therefore concluded that there is a significant difference in the cost effectiveness of service provision between

MCs and SCs among the hard to reach communities and this difference is in favour of MCs.

The implication of these findings is that there should be more investment in MCs than static facilities if the objective of maximizing service utilization by minimizing per contact cost is to be realized in hard to reach Communities.

Cost Effectiveness Ratios				Incremental Cost Effectiveness Ratio		
FACILITY	ANNUAL COST (KSH.)	ANNUAL UTILIZATION	COST EFFECTIVENESS RATIO (CER)	INCREMENTAL COST FOR PAIRED FACILITIES (KSH.)	INCREMENTAL ANNUAL UTILIZATION FOR PAIRED FACILITIES	INCREMENTAL COST EFFECTIVENESS RATIO (ICER)
MC 1	3,494,234	5,153	678.1	1,020,924	4,886	208.9
SC 1	2,473,310	267	9,263			
MC 2	3,645,514	8,018	454.7	1,112,571	5,042	220.7
SC 2	2,532,943	2,976	851.1			
MC 3	2,380,299	4,418	538.8	(95,485)	1,420	(67.2)
SC 3	2,475,784	2,998	825.8			
	$CER = \left(\dfrac{Cost}{Utilization} \right)$			$ICER = \left(\dfrac{Incremental\,Cost}{Incremental\,Utilization} \right)$		

Table 14.2: CERs for Mobile and Static Clinics

14.5 Summary

We have now come to the end of this lecture. In this lecture, we explained the main methods used in Value for Money assessment and discussed the type of questions that each method addresses. We also presented a comparison of the methods. Finally, we presented an illustration on CEA and ICEA for a real project.

14.6 Self-test

To demonstrate your understanding of the methods presented in this lecture, list and explain the main stages involved in each method. This exercise will be done using rotating flip charts followed by directed discussion.

14.7 References and suggestions for further reading

Farida, F. (2013).*Evaluation Methods for Assessing Value for Money*.BetterEvaluation.
Levin,H.M.,&McEwan, P.J.(2001).*Cost-effectiveness-analysis: Methods and applications*. Sage Publications,California.
Rossi, P., Freeman, H.E.,& Lipsey,M.W.(1999). *Evaluation: A Systematic Approach*. Sage Publications, London

LECTURE FIFTEEN: EARNED VALUE ANALYSIS

Lecture Outline

15.1 Introduction

15.2 Lecture Objectives

15.3 Guidelines for Earned Value Management

15.4 Earned Value Analysis

15.5 Summary

15.6 Self-test

15.7 Suggestions for further readings

15.1 Introduction

The interest in and demand for applying and implementing EVM has increased in recent years in government agencies where organizations and auditors are required to report on the adequacy of the organizations internal control over financial reporting (Fleming & Koppelman, 2003, 2010). The private sector has also shown greater interest in applying EVM in recent years with numerous publications promoting EVM principles and advanced project management software packages that incorporate EVM methods and analysis (Anbari, 2003; PMI, 2005).

Earned Value Management (EVM) is a management methodology for integrating scope, schedule and resources and for measuring project performance and progress (Anbari, 2003; Project Management Institute, 2008). EVM is a project management methodology for measuring financial and project performance and has been used under several names, such as earned value project management, earned value method, earned value analysis, and cost/schedule summary report (Fleming & Koppelman, 2003, 2010; Kim, 2000; Kim et.al., 2003).

124

15.2 Lecture Objectives

1. Introduce the concept of Earned Value Management

2. Present the Earned Value Management Guidelines

3. Apply the Earned Value Management to Projects

15.3 Guidelines for Earned Value Management

The American National Standards Institute (ANSI)/Electronic Industries Alliance (EIA) published guidelines for Earned Value Management Systems (EVMS) initially in 1998. The PMI's *PMBOK® Guide* provided the basic terminology and formulas of EVM. In subsequent editions of the *PMBOK® Guide* more detailed and simplified terminology has been presented. PMI has even published a Practice Standard on Earned Value Management. The EVMS guidelines developed by ANSI/EIA identifies 32 criteria that reliable EVM systems should have. These criteria are organized into the following five categories:

Organization:	Activities that define the scope of the effort and assign responsibilities for the work
Planning and Budgeting:	Activities for planning, scheduling, budgeting and authorizing the work
Accounting:	Activities to accumulate the costs of work and material needed to complete the work
Analysis:	Activities to compare budgeted, performed, and actual costs, analyze variances and develop estimates of final costs
Revisions and Data Management:	Activities to incorporate internal and external changes to the scheduled budgeted and authorized work.

15.4 Earned Value Analysis

The traditional variance analysis is backward looking and may be of utility only at the end of the project (post project evaluation). EVM supports both the project manager and the performing contractor because it:

- Provides early identification of adverse trends and potential problems
- Provides an accurate picture of contract status with regard to cost, schedule and status with regard to cost, schedule and technical performance.
- Establishes the baseline for creative actions as needed
- Supports the costs and schedule goals of the customer, project manager and performing contractor.

The traditional variance analysis is the beginning point of EVM. Earned Value (EV) is simply the percent of completed work times the original budget. It is the percent of the original budget that has been earned by actual work completed. It is also called Budgeted Cost of Work Performed. The acronym for this value is BCWP or EV. We now define other variables used in Earned Value Analysis.

Cost Variance (CV) is the difference between the Earned Value and the Actual Costs (AC) also called Actual Cost of Work Performed (ACWP) for the work completed to date. It is calculated as:

$$CV = BCWP - ACWP$$

Schedule Variance (SV) is the difference between the Earned Value to date and the Baseline Schedule. The Baseline Schedule gives the Budgeted Cost of Work Scheduled (BCWS) also called Planned Value, PV. It is calculated thus:

$$SV = BCWP - BCWS$$

Budget variance is the difference between the planned value on the project and actual cost of work performed to date. This variance is useful in calculating the budget burn rate. It is calculated thus:

$$BV = BCWS - ACWP$$

To use EVM, a project baseline ought to be developed. The baseline serves as an anchor point for measuring performance. It is the planned cost and expected schedule performance against which actual cost and schedule are measured. It can also serve as basis for developing cash flows and awarding progress payments. To understand the use of Earned Value Management, follow these reports that we completed after assessing two projects, the first one in Zambia and the other in Uganda:

Example 1:

According to the approved proposal, all the activities for a project were planned to be completed by end of September 2012. A slack time of 6 months was built into the project to bring the end date to March 2013. According to the budget, the planned value (PV) of the project as of 30th September 2012 was K195,320,000, equivalent to the total amount disbursed in tranche 1. For the sake of analysis, this value is referenced as the Budgeted Cost of Work Scheduled (BCWS). However, by the end of September 2012, the amount of work delivered given the budget was K171,600,000. For purposes of analysis, reference this value as Earned Value (EV) or simply as Budgeted Cost of Work Performed (BCWP). This work was delivered at an actual cost of K171,779,867, a figure which we reference as the Actual Cost of Work Performed (ACWP). Given these statistics, the following variances have been calculated:

Cost Variance (CV): This variance measures the difference between the project Earned Value and the Actual Cost of Work Performed. This is expressed thus:

$$CV = BCWP - ACWP = K171,600,000 - K171,779,867$$
$$= -K179,867$$

The implication of this is that the project work has been delivered over budget to the tune of K179,867. Using these statistics, the Cost Performance Index (CPI) which measures the overall project efficiency has been computed thus:

$$CPI = \frac{BCWP}{ACWP} = \frac{K171,600,000}{K171,779,867} = 0.999$$

The implication of this is that every K1 invested into this project has produced K0.999 worth of work which is commendable as it points to close to 100% level of efficiency.

Extending this analysis further, the value of the remaining work to be completed in the next phase is K72,550,000 obtained by adding up the budget costs to the completion period (or simply by subtracting the BCWP from the Budgeted Cost of Total Work (also called Budget At Completion, BAC) for the entire year. If the project continues at the calculated level of efficiency i.e. at 0.999, then the amount needed to execute the remaining work (Estimate To Complete, ETC) is calculated thus:

$$ETC = \frac{BAC - BCWP}{CPI} = \frac{K72,550,000}{0.999} = K72,622,623$$

Thus the final cost to complete this project (Estimate At Completion-EAC) is estimated thus:

$EAC = ETC + ACWP = K244,402,490$ which is higher than the original budget of K244,150,000 implying that at the end of the project, there will be an overrun accounted for by the Variance At Completion (VAC) calculated thus:

$$VAC = BAC - EAC = K244,150,000 - K244,402,490 = -K252,490$$

The implication here is that, *ceteris paribus*, the project will require K252,490 over and above the initial allocation to complete the remaining work. This is not of concern now to

128

the project given that the project has made foreign exchange gains amounting to K3,320,440 determined as the difference between the actual amount received in local currency of K198,640,440 and what should have been received at the budget rate of K5000, i.e. K195,320,000. Indeed, the implication here is that the project will have a surplus of K3,067,950 at the end which translates to US$ 613.60 at the budget rate.

This situation is also further cushioned by the fact that the amount budgeted for utilities i.e K1,200,000 for the period to 30th September 2012 has not been spent. This amount was meant to defray costs related to electricity and water but these are actually included in the K9,000,000 rental payment. As such, the total projected surplus at the end of this project at budget rate is estimated at K5,468,000 made up of K3,068,000 in foreign exchange gain net of the *VAC* and K2,400,000 being the budgeted annual value of utilities. This surplus translates to US$ 1,093.60 at budget rate.

The Budget Burn Rate (BBR) for this project is determined thus:

$$BBR = \frac{BCWS}{ACWP} = \frac{K195,320,000}{K171,779,867} = 1.14$$ implying that to produce K1 of work, the project is putting in K1.14. Given that the project has already completed 6 months and burned K171,779,867 in actual costs, the Time Required (TR) to burn the remaining amount is computed thus:

$$TR = \frac{K72,550,000}{K171,779,867} \times 6 = 2.5$$ Implying that *ceteris paribus* the remaining work will

actually take 2.5 months to complete. This ideally means that the project will be idle from mid November 2012 which challenges the original assumption that this project will take 12 months. Does it make sense that the project staff continue to receive salaries from November 2012 to March 2013 without performing activities traceable to the project?

The Schedule Performance Index (SPI) is obtained thus:

129

$$SPI = \frac{BCWP}{BCWS} = \frac{K171,600,000}{K195,320,440} = 0.88 \text{ implying that for every K1 of work scheduled,}$$

the project has only been able to deliver K0.88 worth of work. Ideally, the project is behind schedule by 12% worth of work scheduled. But this is explained given that the work not delivered is dependent on the availability of a *Drum Resource* at the Ministry of Health. The risk posed by this constraint should have been foreseen at the time of planning and an appropriate resource buffer should have been anticipated and planned into the project.

Example 2

According to the TCA approved budget, the Budgeted Cost of Work Performed (BCWP) totals UGX 49,952,446. The planned value of work as of 30th September 2012 is UGX64,341,000. For the sake of analysis, reference this planned value as the Budgeted Cost of Work Scheduled (BCWS). The actual cost incurred in delivering the performed work is UGX 35,213,136. Using these values, the following statistics are calculated:

Cost Variance (CV) which measures the extent of cost overrun

$$CV = BCWP - ACWP = UGX\,49,952,446 - UGX\,35,213,136 = UGX\,14,739,310$$
implying that this project has been delivered under budget to the tune of the value of this cost variance.

The Cost Performance Index (CPI) is calculated thus:

$$CPI = \frac{BCWP}{ACWP} = \frac{UGX\,49,952,446}{UGX\,35,213,136} = 1.42 \text{ implying that for every UGX1 invested in}$$

this project, the project has been able to churn out UGX1.42 worth of work which points to 142% level of cost efficiency.

Arising from this analysis the amount of the cost variance works to US$6,185.20 at budget rate. This figure is enough to finance the needed sensitization campaigns without asking for variation in scope.

The Schedule Variance (SV) which measures the project effectiveness in meeting targets is determined thus:

$$SV = BCWP - BCWS = UGX\,49,952,446 - UGX\,64,341,000 = -UGX\,14,388,554 \text{ and}$$

the

Schedule Performance Index (SPI) is calculated thus:

$$SPI = \frac{BCWP}{BCWS} = \frac{UGX\,49,952,446}{UGX\,64,341,000} = 0.78$$

These figures imply that the project is behind schedule by UGX14,388,554 worth of work or for every UGX1 of scheduled work, the project has been able to deliver UGX 0.78 worth of work pointing to 78% level of effectiveness.

Ceteris Paribus, the amount of money required to complete the remaining work (ETC) is determined thus:

$$ETC = \frac{Re\,mainingWork}{CPI} = \frac{UGX\,35,027,717}{1.42} = UGX\,24,667,406$$

Therefore, the total cost of this project (EAC) shall be:

$$EAC = ETC + ACWP = UGX\,24,667,406 + UGX\,35,213,136 = UGX\,59,880,542 \text{ which}$$

leads to a Variance At Completion (VAC) of:

$$VAC = EAC - BAC = UGX\,59,880,542 - UGX\,84,980,163 = UGX\,25,099,621 \text{ which}$$

works out to US$ 10,533. The implication here is that this project will be delivered under budget to the tune of US$ 10,533, *ceteris paribus.*

131

Whereas this is commendable, this assessment established that there might be costs that have not been recorded. For example, the recent financial report does not seem to reflect all the costs particularly the amounts of money used up by the TCA management in running this project.

Sometimes the project may not have extra resources and may need to deliver as scheduled or budgeted. In such a case the team should work to recover both lost time and budget. In this case, the CPI required to deliver the remaining work is called To-Complete-Performance Index (TCPI) and is calculated thus:

$$TCPI = \left(\frac{BAC - BCWP}{BAC - ACWP} \right)$$

For instance, if the BAC is Ksh. 7,000,000 and the Earned Value to date is Ksh. 5,000,000. Assuming the Actual Cost of Work Performed is Ksh. 5,500,000. TCPI is computed as follows:

$$TCPI = \frac{7,000,000 - 5,000,000}{7,000,000 - 5,500,000} = 1.3$$ This means that to complete the remaining work, for every Ksh.1 invested, the project should produce work worth Ksh. 1.30 implying 130% level of efficiency.

15.5 Summary

We have now come to the end of this lecture. In this lecture, we introduced you to the concepts of EVM and presented the guidelines for developing an EVMS in your organizations. We then took you through the use of EVA to track project performance.

15.6 Self-test

To demonstrate your understanding of the Earned Value Analysis, explain the factors that you should bear in mind when setting up an EVMS in an organization. What are the main strengths of using EVA to track project performance?

15.7 References and suggestions for further reading

Project Management Institute, (2013), *A Guide to the Project Management Body of Knowledge*, 5th ed. Newton Square, PA: Author

Project Management Institute, (2011), *Practice Standard for Earned Value Management*, Newton Square, PA: Author

Anbari, F.T. (2003). *Earned Value Project Management Method and Extensions*. Project Management Journal, 34(4), 12-23.

Fleming, Q.W. &Koppelman, J.M. (2010).*Earned Value Project Management* (4th Ed.). Newton Square, PA: Project Management Institute

Fleming, Q.W. &Koppelman, J.M. (2003, September). *What is your Project's Real Price Tag?* Harvard Business Review, 81(9), 20-22

KIM, E.H. (2000). *A Study on the effective implementation of earned value management methodology* (Doctoral dissertation).George Washington University, Washington, DC.

KIM, E.H., Wells, W.G.,Jr., &Duffey, M.R. (2003). *A Model for effective implementation of earned value management methodology*. International Journal of Project Management, 21(5), 375-382

LECTURE SIXTEEN: INTRODUCTION TO PROJECT RISK ASSESSMENT

Lecture Outline

16.1 Introduction

16.2 Lecture Objectives

16.3 Rationale for assessing risk on projects

16.4 Individual/organizational attitudes towards risks

16.5 Types of project risks

16.6Steps in risk management

16.7 Summary

16.8 Self-test

16.9 Suggestions for further reading

16.1 Introduction

This lecture is a continuation of lecture one. Therefore, you are asked to revisit lecture one to ensure that you are comfortable with the presentation on early warning signs before proceeding to this lecture.

16.2 Lecture Objectives

1. Define the concepts of risk and risk management

2. Explain the various individual/organizational attitudes towards risk

3. Present the various processes involved in project risk management

16.3 Rationale for assessing risks on projects

Project risk is an uncertain event or condition that, if it occurs, has a positive or negative effect on a Project's objectives. Project objectives include benefits, scope, schedule, cost

134

and quality. Risk is the effect of uncertainty on achievement of project objectives. According to the *PMBOK® Guide* (2013) Project Risk Management includes the processes concerned with conducting risk management planning, identification, analysis, responses and monitoring and control on a project. The objectives of project risk management are to increase the probability and impact of positive events and decrease the probability and impact of negative events in the project. Project Risk Management aims to identify and prioritize risks in advance of the occurrence, and provide action oriented information to Project Managers. This orientation requires consideration of events that may or may not occur and are therefore described in terms of likelihood or probability of occurrence in addition to other dimensions such as their impact on objectives.

The purpose of risk management is to identify, assess and control uncertainty and, as a result, improve the ability of the project to succeed. Risk-taking in projects is inevitable since projects are enablers of change and change introduces uncertainty; hence risk (Kerzner, 2008). Management of risk is about the proactive identification, assessment and control of risks that may affect the delivery of the project's objectives. Management of risk is a continual activity, performed throughout the life of the project *(ibid)*. According to the PRINCE2® Manual (2009), for risk management to be effective, risks must be identified, assessed and controlled. When a risk event occurs, it ceases to become uncertain. Threats which occur may be called issues or problems; opportunities which occur may be called benefits.

According to the PMI *Practice Standard for Project Risk Management* (2009), project risk can be classified as either individual or overall risk. Individual risks are specific events or conditions that might affect project objectives, elements or tasks. Understanding individual risks can assist in determining how to apply effort and resources to enhance the chances of project success. Day to day project risk management focuses on these individual risks in order to enhance the prospects of a successful project outcome. Overall project risk represents the effect of uncertainty on the project as a whole. Overall project risk is more than the sum of individual risks on a project since it applies to the whole project rather than individual elements or tasks. It represents the exposure of stakeholders to the implications of variations in project outcome. It is an important component of strategic decision-making, program or portfolio management and project governance where investments are sanctioned or cancelled and priorities are set.

The M&E practitioner interacts with risk management as follows:

- Determining the acceptable levels of risk for the Project in consultation with stakeholders.
- Checking that the recommended risk responses have been implemented successfully
- Checking that the contingency funds were applied adequately in responding to the risks that occurred
- Regularly reporting risk status to key stakeholders with recommendations for appropriate strategic decisions and actions to maintain acceptable risk exposure.
- Escalating identified risks to senior management where possible.
- Monitoring the efficiency and effectiveness of the project risk management process.
- Auditing risk responses for their effectiveness and documenting lessons learned.

16.4 Individual/organizational attitudes towards risks
Based on the PMI *Practice Standard for Project Risk Management* (2009), the risk attitudes of the project stakeholders determine the extent to which an individual risk or overall project risk matters. It is important that professionals involved in monitoring and evaluation understand their clients' attitudes to risk since the recommendations they make must be aligned to the organization's risk attitude. A wide range of factors influence risk attitude. These include:

136

- Risk appetite which is the degree of uncertainty an entity is willing to take on in anticipation of a reward
- Risk tolerance which is the degree, amount or volume of risk that an organization or individual will withstand
- Risk threshold which refers to measures along the level of uncertainty or the level of impact at which a stakeholder may have a specific interest. Below that threshold the organization will accept the risk and above the risk threshold the organization will not tolerate the risk.
- The scale of the project within the range of stakeholders overall activities
- The strength of public commitments made about the performance of the project
- The stakeholders' sensitivity to issues such as environmental impacts, industrial relations and other factors

Stakeholders risk attitudes usually result in a desire for increased certainty in project outcomes, and may express a preference for one project objective over another.

How risk is regarded is usually also strongly influenced by an organization's culture. Different organizations are more or less open, and this often impacts the way risk management can be applied. These attitudes should be identified and managed proactively and deliberately through the project risk management process. Stakeholder attitudes to risk are classified as follows:

Risk taker attitude: This is also called risk seeking attitude. Risk takers attach more weight to a dollar gained compared to a dollar lost. Risk seekers understand very well that the probability of climbing Mt. Everest to the top and then back down is less than 0.5 and that the cost of climbing this mountain ranges in millions of US dollars. Yet the list of those who want to climb the mountain is ever growing!

Risk averse attitude: Risk aversion involves attaching more weight to a dollar lost compared to a dollar gained. Risk averse organizations require higher compensation to take on an extra unit of risk. In other words, they build protective structures around what they already own and only when they ensure that it is quite safe is when they take on any initiatives that are risky. In any case, they must get commensurate return.

Risk neutral attitude: Organizations or stakeholders exhibiting this attitude to risk are indifferent to different risk levels and attach same weight to a shilling gained and lost. It is not easy to find organizations or stakeholders who are risk neutral. Most of them will be either risk seekers or risk averse.

Think about your organization/host institution or context. Identify the applicable risk attitude. Explain your choice.

16.5 Types of risk

The total risk in a project or activity before applying any risk treatment strategy is usually called inherent risk. In an attempt to handle inherent risk on a project, we usually implement some response or work around strategy. This could totally eradicate the risk or simply reduce its likelihood of occurrence and/or impact on project objectives. When the strategy deployed cannot totally eradicate the risk, the risk that remains is referred to as systematic or residual risk, sometimes also referred to as idiosyncratic risk. This residual risk is what should be the key concern of project management and thus monitoring and evaluation.

When projects are managed as a portfolio or program, each individual project has its own inherent risk commonly referred to as standalone risk. The combined standalone risks of individual projects in a program or portfolio comprise the overall program or portfolio risk. Usually, when projects are held in a portfolio, the overall resultant weighted risk is lower than the sum of the individual standalone risks.

Some risk is said to be diversified away as a result of holding projects in a portfolio since negative risk values on one project cancel out with positive risk values for another project in the portfolio. Thus holding projects in a portfolio is said to be a risk diversification strategy. The portion of the overall risk that disappears as a result of holding projects in a portfolio is called diversifiable or unsystematic risk. The remaining portion of risk is the systematic or market risk. Again, it is this market risk that the portfolio manager/monitoring and evaluation should be concerned with.

It is possible that implementing a primary risk handling strategy on a project can lead to another risk. This is why risk identification is said to be continuous on the project. Project monitoring is about assessing the performance of the risk response plan while looking for any new risks that may have escaped identification during project planning. Suppose you employ a watchman to take watch over project assets. You do this to control the risk of theft of the assets.

Assume you have also installed CCTV cameras to capture all movements including thieves. Since the watchman knows this, he may not always spend the entire night at the project or he may not be awake the whole night. When thieves observe such behavior in the watchman, they plan to strike when he is either away or asleep. They can cause blackout so that they are not captured by the cameras. There is a secondary risk caused by the watchman's assumption that even he is away or asleep, the cameras will scare aware thieves. To deal with this secondary risk, you may intensify supervision visits to the project at night to ensure that the watchman is present and is awake. This intensified supervision is a form of work around strategy.

 Can you think of other examples of secondary risks from your context?

16.6 Risk Management Processes

In order to effectively monitor and evaluate project risk, it is important that you understand and apply the processes involved in risk management. Notice that there are times when you may be called upon to evaluate the risk management processes either within an organization or on a project. Generally, the ISO 21500 documents four main risk management processes as follows:

- Identify risks process
- Assess risks process
- Treat risks process
- Control risks process

PRINCE2® methodology recommends the use of five risk management processes namely:

- Identify risks process
- Assess risks process
- Plan risk response process
- Implement risk response process
- Communicate risk process

The *PMBOK® Guide* (2013) documents processes that should be followed in the management of risk on projects. These are:

- Plan risk management process
- Identify risks process
- Perform qualitative risk analysis
- Perform quantitative risk analysis
- Plan risk response process
- Monitor and control risks

We have chosen to follow the *PMBOK® Guide* processes because they address both the ISO 21500 and PRINCE2® processes. A brief description of these processes is presented below. For a more comprehensive account of these processes, refer to the *PMBOK*[®] *Guide* (2013).

(i) Plan Risk Management Process

This process should begin when a project is conceived and should be completed early during project planning. Its main output is the risk management plan. The main sections of the risk management plan are: Project Title and Date of Preparation of the Plan, Methods and Approaches to Risk Management, Tools and Techniques to be used in Risk Management, Roles and Responsibilities in Risk Management, Risk Categories, Stakeholder Risk Tolerance, Definitions of Probability, Definitions of Impact, Probability and Impact Matrix, Risk Management Funding, Contingency Protocols, Frequency and Timing of Risk events, Risk Audit approach, Templates such as Risk Register, Risk Hit Map, Risk Break Down Structure etc.

(ii) Identify Risks Process

This process involves determining which risks may affect the project and documenting their characteristics. The tools and techniques used to identify risks include: Document Reviews, Internet Exploration, Delphi Technique, Brainstorming, Interviewing (Key stakeholders, Past Project Managers and Task Managers), SWOT Analysis, Checklists, Assumption and Constraint Analysis, Diagramming Techniques (Flow charts, Decision trees), Cause and Effect Analysis (Failure Mode and Effect Analysis, Fish borne/Ishikawa diagrams, Root Cause analysis, K-J Analysis), Influence Diagrams, Scenario and Sensitivity Analysis, Expert judgment etc.

Following this process, a preliminary risk register is constructed containing a list of risks. A risk register is a document that contains results of various risk management processes, often displayed in a table or spreadsheet format. It is a tool for documenting potential risk events and related information. The risk register includes the following main headings: An identification number for each risk event, a rank for each risk event, the name of the risk event, a description of the risk event, the category under which the risk event falls

141

(risk categories are usually shown using Risk Breakdown Structure-RBS. RBS presents a structured way of communicating risks and can be used as a risk governance model to help in monitoring and controlling risks), the root cause of the risk event, triggers for each risk event (triggers are indicators or symptoms of actual risk events), potential responses to each risk event, the risk owner, or person who will own or take responsibility for the risk event, the probability of the risk event occurring, the impact to the project if the risk event occurs, the status of the risk event. (N/B: we will later in this chapter show a risk register and RBS for a typical project).

Risks are identified continuously on the project and the monitoring and evaluation practitioner needs to understand the techniques used in risk identification so as to be able to identify emergent and secondary risks.

(iii) Perform Qualitative & Quantitative Risk Assessment Process

Risk identification produces a list of potential risks. Not all of these risks deserve attention. Some are trivial and can be ignored, while others poise serious threats to the welfare of the project. Managers have to develop methods for sifting through the list of risks eliminating inconsequential or redundant ones and stratifying worthy ones in terms of importance and need for attention. Risk assessment can be done using a broad range of techniques including quantitative and qualitative techniques.

The main tools and techniques used in qualitative risk analysis include risk probability and impact assessment, probability and impact matrix, risk data quality assessment, risk categorization, risk urgency assessment and expert judgment. Quantitative techniques used to analyze risks include scenario analysis, ratio/range analysis, failure mode and effect analysis, sensitivity analysis, Delphi method, decision tree analysis, utility theory, decision theory, Monte Carlo simulation etc. We will later in this chapter demonstrate the use of the failure mode and effect analysis and the Risk Hit Map.

142

(iv) Plan Risk Responses process

When a risk event is identified and assessed, a decision must be made concerning which response is appropriate for the specific event. Risk handling includes specific methods and techniques to deal with known risks, identifies who is responsible for the risk issue, and provides and provides an estimate of the resources associated with handling the risk, if any. It involves planning and execution with the objective of reducing risks to an acceptable level.

There are several factors that can influence our response to a risk, including but not limited to:

- Amount and quality of information on the actual hazards that caused the risk (descriptive uncertainty)
- Amount and quality of information on the magnitude of the damage (measurement uncertainty)
- Personal benefit to project manager for accepting the risk (voluntary risk)
- Risk forced upon the project manager (involuntary risk)
- The existence of cost-effective alternatives (equitable risks)
- The existence of high-cost alternatives or possibly lack of options (inequitable risks)
- Length of exposure to the risk

Risk handling must be compatible with the Risk management plan and any additional guidance the program manager provides. Personnel that evaluate candidate risk handling strategies may use the following criteria as a starting point for evaluation:

- Can the strategy be feasibly implemented and still meet the user's needs?
- What is the expected effectiveness of the handling strategy in reducing program risk to an acceptable level?
- Is the strategy affordable in terms of dollars and other resources (e.g., use of critical materials and test facilities)?
- Is time available to develop and implement the strategy and what effect does that have on the overall program schedule?
- What effect does the strategy have on the system's technical performance?

Using the Risk Heat Map, some risks are transferred to the watch-list to be monitored but others are automatically assigned a response plan. Based on the *PMBOK® Guide* (2013), the risk handling strategies can be categorized as follows:

- Avoid a threat or Exploit an opportunity.
- Transfer a threat or share an opportunity.
- Mitigate a threat or enhance an opportunity.
- Accept a threat or an opportunity.

We will discuss each of these strategies in detail in a later lecture.

(v) *Control Risks Process*

This is the process of implementing risk response plans, tracking identified risks, monitoring residual risks, identifying new risks and evaluating risk process effectiveness throughout the project. This is done in order to optimize risk responses across the project life cycle (*PMBOK® Guide*, 2013). This process is key in determining if:

- Project assumptions are still valid
- Analysis shows an assessed risk has changed or can be retired
- Risk management policies and procedures are being followed
- Contingency reserves for cost or schedule should be modified in alignment with current risk assessment

This process uses risk audits to examine and document the effectiveness of risk responses in dealing with identified risks and their root causes as well as the effectiveness of the risk management process. Most risk monitoring and evaluation work is done during this process.

Relate this to your own experience and context: find out whether your organization/host institution follows the processes recommended by ISO 21500, *PMBOK® Guide* or PRINCE®. If other, please explain briefly.

16.7 Summary

We have now come to the end of this lecture. In this lecture, we introduced you to the concepts of risk and risk management by explaining the rationale for conducting project risk management. We then explained the various individual and organizational attitudes towards risk. This was followed with a presentation on the various types of project risks. We have ended the lecture with a discussion of the risk management

16.8 Self-test

Imagine that your organization or host institution has no risk policy or framework in place. You are helping them develop these and you have called senior management to a meeting to help them identify their attitude towards risk as a starting point. Develop a one-page write-up that you will use to explain to them why they need to understand their risk attitude.

16.9 Suggestions for further reading

AXELOS Ltd.-OGC. (2009). *Managing Successful Projects with PRINCE2™*.The Stationery Office, UK.
Kerzner, H. (2008).*Project Management-A Systems Approach to Planning, Scheduling, and Controlling*(10th Edition). John Wiley & Sons Inc.
Project Management Institute, (2013), *A Guide to the Project Management Body of Knowledge*,(5th ed.).Newton Square, PA: Author
Project Management Institute, (2009), *Practice Standard for Project Risk Management*, Newton Square, PA: Author

LECTURE SEVENTEEN: QUALITATIVE AND QUANTITATIVE RISK EVALUATION

Lecture Outline

17.1 Introduction

17.2 Lecture Objectives

17.3 Distinction between qualitative and quantitative risk evaluation

17.3 Qualitative risk evaluation techniques

17.4 Quantitative risk evaluation techniques

17.5 Recommend an appropriate risk response

17.6 Summary

17.7 Self-test

17.8 References and suggestions for further reading

17.1 Introduction

This lecture is a continuation from the previous one and involves a presentation of processes 3 and 4 of the *PMBOK* Guide (2013) Project Risk Management Knowledge Area. In this lecture, we distinguish between qualitative and quantitative risk assessment with the intention of determining the value of the risk

17.2 Lecture Objectives

1. Distinguish between qualitative and quantitative risk analysis

2. Present the tools and techniques used in conducting qualitative and quantitative analysis

3. Illustrate the use of these tools and techniques

146

17.3 Distinction between qualitative and quantitative risk evaluation

The project risk management plan or framework usually defines the organization's risk profile or appetite and determines how the likelihood of occurrence and impact of various risk events can be assessed and characterized. Usually, risks can be characterized as being high, medium or low in terms of either likelihood of occurrence or impact. The risk management plan will provide a working definition of what is high, medium or low and will provide guidelines to the interpretation of risk data. According to the PMI's Practice Standard for Project Risk Management (2009), risk identification produces a list of potential risks. Not all of these risks deserve attention. Some are trivial and can be ignored, while others poise serious threats to the welfare of the project. Managers have to develop methods for sifting through the list of risks eliminating inconsequential or redundant ones and stratifying worthy ones in terms of importance and need for attention. Risk assessment can be done using a broad range of techniques including quantitative and qualitative techniques. These techniques are distinguished in the PMI[R] Practice Standard for Risk Management (2009) as shown below:

Qualitative	Quantitative
<ul><li>Addresses individual risks descriptively.</li><li>Assesses the discrete probability of occurrence and impact on objectives if it does occur.</li><li>Prioritizes individual risks for subsequent treatment.</li><li>Adds to risk register.</li><li>Leads to quantitative Risk Analysis.</li></ul>	<ul><li>Predicts likely project outcomes based on combined effects of risks.</li><li>Uses probability distributions to characterize the risk's probability and impact.</li><li>Uses project model e.g. schedule cost estimate.</li><li>Uses quantitative methods, requires specialized tools.</li><li>Estimates likelihood of meeting targets and contingency needed to achieve desired level of comfort.</li><li>Identifies risks with greatest effect on overall project risk.</li></ul>

Table 14.1: Qualitative and Quantitative Risk Analysis

17.3 Qualitative risk evaluation techniques

In qualitative risk evaluation, risks are assessed descriptively and qualitatively as being high, medium or low in probability and impact. The main tools and techniques used in qualitative risk analysis include risk probability and impact assessment, probability and impact matrix, risk data quality assessment, risk categorization, risk urgency assessment and expert judgment. The output of this process is updates to the risk register through a prioritized list of risks.

Illustration 1: Qualitative Risk Analysis

The Risk Breakdown Structure (RBS) for a project we were involved in addressing fight against AIDS is shown below:

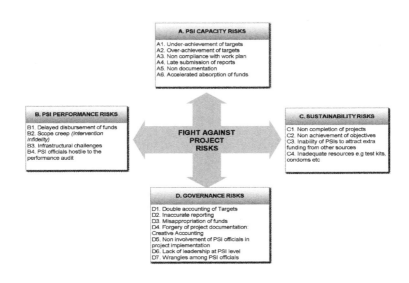

Figure 17.1: Risk Breakdown Structure for HIV/AIDS Scourge

Based on this RBS, the qualitative analysis of these risks is shown in the table below:

Risk ID	Risk Description	Risk Trigger	Likelihood of occurrence	Impact on PDC	Exposure	Detection Difficulty	Risk Value	Risk Status
A1	Under-achievement of targets	Achievement less than approved	High	High	High	High	High	
A2	Over-achievement of targets	Achievement more than approved	Low	High	Medium	Medium	Medium	
A3	Noncompliance with work plan	Over-expenditure, unapproved activities	High	High	High	High	High	
A4	Late submission of reports	Overdue reports	High	Medium	Medium	Medium	Medium	
A5	Non documentation	Incomplete or no support documents	High	High	High	High	High	
A6	Accelerated absorption of funds	Budget exhausted earlier than approved	Medium	High	Medium	Low	Low	
B1	Delayed disbursement of funds	PSI receives funds long after approval	Medium	High	Medium	Medium	Medium	
B2	Scope creep	Unapproved activities	Low	High	Medium	High	Medium	
B3	Infrastructural challenges	Poor/bad terrain	High	Medium	Medium	Low	Low	
B4	Project sub-implementers' (PSIs) officials hostile to auditors	Officials evade auditors or hide documents	Low	High	Medium	High	Medium	
C1	Non completion of projects	Stalled projects	Low	High	Medium	High	Medium	
C2	Non achievement of objectives	Under-achievement of targets	High	High	High	High	High	
C3	Inability of PSIs to attract extra funding from other sources	PSIs rely only on current project funding	High	High	High	Low	Medium	
C4	Inadequate resources	Stock-outs in supplies e.g. test kits, condoms	Medium	High	Medium	Low	Low	
D1	Double accounting of Targets	Reports reflect achievements of other funding	Low	High	Medium	High	Medium	

150

Risk ID	Risk Description	Risk Trigger	Likelihood of occurrence	Impact on PDC	Exposure	Detection Difficulty	Risk Value	Risk Status
D2	Inaccurate reporting	Unsupported reports by source documents	Low	High	Medium	High	Medium	
D3	Misappropriation of funds	Funds misdirected	Low	High	Medium	High	Medium	
D4	Forgery of project documentation	Documents certified as unauthentic	Low	High	Medium	High	Medium	
D5	Noninvolvement of PSI officials	Signatories to the sub-financing agreement not involved	Medium	Medium	Medium	Low	Low	
D6	Lack of leadership at PSI level	Lack of clear vision and mission	Medium	High	Medium	Low	Low	
D7	Wrangles among PSI officials	Splinter groups/camps among members	Medium	High	Medium	Medium	Medium	

Table 17.2: Risk Assessment for a Project to fight HIV/AIDS Scourge

Based on this qualitative analysis of the risks, the criticality and profile of these risks is presented in the following Risk Hit Map (RHM) which shows the typology of risk by mapping the relationship that exists between the likelihood that the risk will occur and the impact that the occurrence of the risk will have on the Project Delivery Capability, PDC. It is from the RHM that risks that require contingency planning and those that require to be included on the watch list are identified.

TOWA PROJECT RISK HEAT MAP

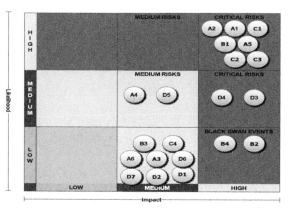

Figure 17.2: Risk Hit Map

Black Swan events represent highly improbable but high impact risks. The chance that they will occur is highly remote but if they occur they can bring down the entire project. For example the probability of an airplane crashing is very low but the impact is disastrous. Such an event is described as Black Swan. It is said that it is such events that caused the recent world economic recession.

From the RHM presented above, indicate which region(s) fall within the risk tolerance line.

17.4 Quantitative risk evaluation techniques

Qualitative risk evaluation develops a prioritized list of risks. On the basis of this list, some risks can be said to HH (High Probability-High Impact), HM (High Probability-Medium Impact) etc. Quantitative risk analysis uses the prioritized list of risks to subject the risks to quantitative analysis. Usually the risk management plan or framework will

152

explain quantitative scales and measures of risk and impact. It will also explain how to determine the value of risk.

There are several tools and techniques used in quantitative risk evaluation. Clifford & Erick (2003), Kerzner (2006) and the *PMBOK® Guide* (2013) explain these as follows:

(i) Scenario Analysis

Scenario analysis is the easiest and most commonly used technique for analyzing risks. Team members assess each risk in terms of:

- The undesirable events
- All the outcomes of the event's occurrence
- The magnitude or severity of the event's impact
- Chances/probability of the events happening
- When the event might occur in the project
- Interaction with other parts of this or other projects.

Documentation of scenario analyses can be seen in various risk assessment forms used by organizations. The table below is a partial example of a risk assessment form (Risk severity Matrix)

Risk Event	Risk Severity Descriptors				Risk Value (RE X DD)	When will the risk be detected
	Likelihood of risk occurring (L)	Impact of risk on project (I)	Risk Exposure (RE)= (L X I)	Detection Difficulty (DD)		
Money laundering	4	4	16	4	64	Execution
Targets not achieved	2	5	10	5	50	Execution
Unsatisfied users	4	3	12	3	36	Monitoring
Non documentation	1	5	5	5	25	Execution

Table 17.3: Partial Example of a Risk Assessment Form

Often organizations find it useful to categorize the severity of different risks into some form of risk assessment matrix. The matrix is typically structured around the impact and likelihood of the risk event with each element representing a different set of impact and likelihood values.

(ii) Ratio/Range Analysis

This technique is also widely used by project managers. The technique uses data from prior projects that are similar to the proposed project. It assumes a ratio between the old and new project to make a point estimate of the time, cost or technology and allow high range of estimate. The ratio typically serves as a constant. For example, if past projects have taken 10minutes per line of computer code, a constant of 1.10 [which represents a 10 percent increase] would be used for the proposed project time estimates because the new project will be more difficult than prior projects. Given the computed estimate for the new project, the percentage ranges for past projects can also be reviewed and the downside risk of the range assessed.

(iii)Failure Mode and Effect Analysis [FMEA]

This quality tool is a variation of the risk severity matrix discussed earlier. Each risk is assessed in terms of the following score:

Impact x Probability x Detection difficulty= Risk value

Each of the three dimensions is rated according to a five-point scale. For example, detection is defined as the ability of the project team to discern that the risk event is imminent. A score of 1 would be given if the risk is too easy to spot. The highest detection score of 5 would be given to events that could only be discovered after it is too late. Similar anchored scales would be applied for severity of impact and the probability of the event occurring. The weighting of the risks is then based on their overall score. For example, a risk with an impact in the "1" zone with a very low probability and an easy detection score might score a 1 [1x 1 x1 =1].

Conversely, high-impact risk with a high probability and impossible to detect would score 125 [5x 5 x5 =125]. This broad range of numerical scores allows for easy stratification of risk according to overall significance.

154

(iv)Sensitivity Analysis.

Sensitivity analysis seeks to place a value on the effect of change of a single variable within a project by analyzing the effect on the project plan. It is the simplest form of risk analysis. Uncertainty and risk are reflected by defining a likely range of variation for each component of the original base case estimate. In practice such analysis is only done for those variables which have impact on cost, time or economic return, and to which the project will be most sensitive. The effect of change of each of these variables on the final cost or time criteria is then assessed in turn across the assumed ranges.

If several variables are changed, the most sensitive or critical variable can be compared graphically in a sensitivity diagram. Some of the advantages of sensitivity analysis include impressing the management that there is a range of possible outcomes, decision making is more realistic, though perhaps more complex, and the relative importance of each variable examined is readily apparent. Some weaknesses are that variables are treated individually, limiting the extent to which combinations of variables be assessed, and a sensitivity diagram gives no identification of anticipated probability of occurrence.

In your opinion, what is the difference between scenario and sensitivity analysis as used in risk evaluation?

(v) Delphi Method.

The basic concept of the Delphi method is to derive a consensus using a panel of experts to arrive at a convergent solution to a specific problem. This is particularly useful, for example, in arriving at probability assessment relating to future events where the risk

155

impact is large and critical. The first and vital step is to select a panel of individuals, as participants, who have experience in the area at issue, for best results the panel members should not know each other's identity and the process should be conducted with each in separate locations. This is to prevent single member influence and simplistic occurrence.

A scenario is established and each panelist is requested to reply to a questionnaire. The responses, together with opinions and justifications, are evaluated and statistical feedback is furnished to each panel member in the next iteration. The process is continued until group response coverage to a specific solution. Should the responses diverge, the facilitator needs to review the wording of the questionnaire, the feedback, or the experience of the panelists to determine if there is a problem which needs to be corrected.

(vi) **Decision Tree Analysis**.

A feature of project work is that a number of options are typically available in the course of reaching the final results. Indeed, even before considering the project in any detail or developing a network analysis for example, the decision maker is faced with an array of procurement possibilities and a sequence of decision choices. The Decision Tree provides a graphical means of bringing the information together.

An advantage in its application to risk analysis is that it forces consideration of the probability of each outcome. Thus, the likelihood of failures is quantified and some value is placed on each decision. This form of risk analysis is usually applied to cost and time consideration, both in choosing between different early investments decision and later in considering major changes with certain outcomes during project implementation.

In the latter case, it may be linked to a sensitivity analysis as a means of determining the value of a certain decision.

(vii) **Utility Theory**

None of the techniques discussed so far takes into account the attitude towards risk of the decision maker. It may be reasonable to suppose, for example, that a potential loss of 90% would not be viewed with the same equanimity as, say a loss of 10%. Somewhere in between the attitude will change. However, at what point may well depend on the attitude of the decision maker. That is to say, the decision maker may be risk seeking, risk neutral or risk averse.

Utility Theory endeavors to formalize management's attitude towards risk, an approach which is appropriate to Decision Tree Analysis for the calculation of expected values, and also for the assessment of results from sensitivity and probability analyses. However, in practical project work Utility Theory tends to be viewed as theoretical.

(viii) **Decision Theory.**

Decision Theory is a technique for assisting in reaching decisions under uncertainty and risk. All decisions are based to some extent on uncertain forecasts. Given the criteria selected by the decision maker, Decision Theory points to the best possible course whether or not the forecasts are accurate. Event probabilities can often be estimated using statistical inferences based on history. Severity of consequences may be similarly derived or by estimating the impact of specific events by developing resulting scenarios. Expected value (EV) can be used to adjust the value of the consequences of any given outcome for the probability of its occurrence.

Assume that you are working on a project which has an estimated cost of $90,000 and has to be completed in 31 days. In addition, there is a $50,000 penalty if completion takes longer. How significant is this risk? Assume that based on the most risky path there is an 88% chance of completing the project in 31 days or less; therefore, there is a 12% chance that the project would not be completed in 31 days. The expected cost is calculated as the

157

sum of the products of the value of an outcome times the probability that that outcome will occur as follows:

Outcome	Value of outcome	Probability	Product
Complete in 31 days or less	$90,000 X	.88 =	$79,200
Complete in more than 31 days	140,000 X	.12 =	16,800
		Expected Value =	$96,000

From this calculation it will be seen that the EV of the cost is substantially higher than the cost and the calculation provides a clearer basis for management decision as, for example a decision as to whether or not to invest in an R&D project. The calculation also provides a basis for other comparative calculations. For instance, whether or not a schedule slippage calculation beyond the 31 days point is a high risk or a low one depends on the consequences that may result in real world terms, it may also depend on who is responsible on this slippage.

(ix) Monte Carlo Simulation

The Monte Carlo method simulation by means of random numbers provides a powerful yet simple method of incorporating probabilistic data. The basic steps are:

- Assess the range for the variables being considered and determine the probability distribution most suited to each.
- For each variable within its specific range, select a value randomly chosen, taking into account of the probability distribution for the occurrence of the variable. This may be achieved by generating the cumulative frequency curve for the variable and choosing a value from random number table.
- Run a deterministic analysis using the combination of values selected for each one of the variables

158

- Repeat steps 2 and 3 a number a times to obtain the probability distribution of the results. The number of iterations required depends on the number of variables and the degree of confidence required, but typically lies between 100 and 1000.

The Monte Carlo process, as applied to risk management, is an attempt to create a series of probability distributions for potential risk items, randomly sample these distributions, and then transform these numbers into useful information that reflects quantification of associated cost, performance, or schedule risks. While often used in technical applications (e.g. integrated circuit performance, structural response to an earthquake), Monte Carlo simulations have been used to estimate risk in the design of service centers; time to complete key milestone in a project; the cost of developing, fabricating and maintaining an item; inventory management; and thousands of other applications (Kerzner, 2008).

The output of the quantitative risk assessment is an update to the prioritized list of risks developed during the perform qualitative risk analysis process.

Write down the strengths and weaknesses of each of the risk evaluation techniques discussed in this section.

Illustration 2: Quantitative Risk Analysis

Follow through this illustration to understand how to undertake quantitative risk analysis. This is another project implemented in over ten countries in Africa that we were involved in. The project was meant to address the tobacco menace.

Following the various assessments we conducted on the performance of the project grantees across Africa, we developed a Risk Breakdown Structure (RBS) as shown below:

159

Category A Risks: Financial Management		Category B Risks: Procedural		Category C Risks: Sustainability	
A.1	High FX Losses	B.1	Non Compliance	C.1	Non Achievement of Targets
A.2	Non Documentation			C.2	Discontinuity
A.3	Financial Manipulation				
A.4	Double Accounting				
A.5	Cash Handling				

Table 17.4: ATCC Risk Breakdown Structure

The triggers (causes) of these risks were documented based on the assessments' findings and each trigger was assessed based on three dimensions namely; Likelihood, Impact and Exposure. These dimensions are defined thus:

- Likelihood: Number of grantees exhibiting risk trigger divided by the total number of grantees
- Impact: The effect of the risk on the attainment of project objectives
- Exposure: The Risk Value i.e. the product of Likelihood and Impact

Values for the Likelihood dimension are based on a scale of 0-1 while the Impact dimension is based on a scale of 1-3. The values of these dimensions together with the resultant values of Exposure dimension are interpreted based on the following scale:

Likelihood	Impact	Exposure	Interpretation
0.00-0.49	1	Below 0.74	Low
0.50-0.69	2	0.74-1.69	Medium
0.70-1.00	3	Above 1.70	High

Table 17.5: Interpretation of the Risk Dimensions

A simplified form of the Failure Mode and Effect Analysis (FMEA) is shown in Table 17.6. The table was filled based on the risks that had actually occurred and identifies the grantees exhibiting specific triggers of the risk. Based on the results in Table 17.6, the project had high exposure to the following risks:

- A.2.1 Non Documentation: Missing Documents with a Risk Value of 2
- A.4.1 Double Accounting: Non Separation of Donor Funds with a Risk Value of 1.7
- B.1.4 Non Compliance: No Back-up System in Place with a Risk Value of 1.7
- C.1.1 Non Achievement of Targets: Strong Tobacco Industry with a Risk Value of 2.7

These risks are shown on the Risk Hit Map (RHM) in Figure 17.3 as being outside the Risk Tolerance Line (High Probability-Medium Impact, High Probability-High Risk, Medium Probability-High Impact). For purposes of sustainability, the post project Benefits Review Plan must be updated to reflect how these risks shall be managed. The RHM also identifies another category of risks which are usually neglected but their occurrence has devastating effects on the project:

- A.3.4 Financial Manipulation: Dishonest Management with a Risk Value of 0.66
- C.2.2 Discontinuity: One Key Man runs the organization with a Risk Value of 1.30

These risks are characterized by Low Likelihood of occurrence but with very High Impact on project objectives should they occur. These are technically referred to as Black Swan Events and will need to be planned into the post project Benefits Review Plan.

Risk Category	Risk Description	Risk Cause	Likelihood	Impact	Exposure	Grantee Exhibiting Risk								
						A	B	C	D	E	F	G	H	I
Financial management	High FX losses (A.1)	Poor financial planning (A.1.1)	0.22	2	0.44	✓			✓					
"A"	No documents (A.2)	Missing documents (A.2.1)	1.00	2	2.00	✓	✓	✓	✓	✓	✓	✓	✓	✓
		No bank reconciliations (A.2.2)	0.67	1	0.67		✓	✓		✓	✓	✓		✓
		No asset register (A.2.3)	0.56	1	0.56			✓			✓	✓		✓
		Lack of policies (A.2.3)	0.33	1	0.33			✓			✓			✓
	Financial manipulation (A.3)	Use of excel spreadsheet (A.3.1)	0.33	2	0.66			✓					✓	✓
		Unauthorized alteration of entries (A.3.2)	0.22	2	0.44					✓			✓	
		One sole account signatory (A.3.3)	0.11	2	0.22						✓			
		Dishonest management (A.3.4)	0.22	3	0.66				✓				✓	
		Unauthorized expenditure (A.3.5)	0.44	2	0.66			✓	✓	✓		✓	✓	✓
	Double accounting (A.4)	Non separation of donor accounting (A.4.1)	0.56	3	1.70	✓						✓		
	Cash handling (A.5)	Lack of a Safe (A.5.1)	0.33	1	0.33			✓			✓	✓	✓	
		All payments done in cash (A.5.2)	0.56	2	1.10			✓		✓	✓	✓	✓	✓
Procedural "B"	Non compliance	Non remittance of statutory	0.44	2	0.88			✓					✓	✓

(B.1)		deductions (B.1.1)			
		Non adherence to existing policies (B.1.2)	0.33	2	0.66
		Lack of staff payroll (B.1.3)	0.67	1	0.67
		No back-up system in place (B.1.4)	0.56	3	1.70
Sustainability "C"	Non achievement of targets (C.1)	Strong tobacco industry interference (C.1.1)	0.89	3	2.70
		Lack of commitment among stakeholders/government (C.1.2)	0.33	3	0.99
	Discontinuity (C.2)	Reliance on one donor (C.2.1)	0.56	2	1.10
		One "Key man" runs the organization (C.2.2)	0.44	3	1.30
		No succession planning (C.2.3)	0.22	2	0.44
		Inconsistent Board meetings (C.2.4)	0.11	2	0.22
		No minutes of Board meetings taken (C.2.5)	0.11	1	0.11

Table 17.6: Failure Mode and Effect Analysis

163

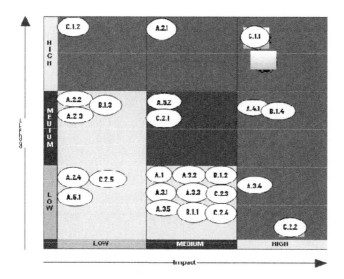

Figure 17.3: Project Risk Heat Map

17.5 Recommending Risk Response

As a monitoring and evaluation practitioner, it is important that you understand the various strategies and responses that are used to handle project risk. At times, you are required to evaluate whether the risk response strategies that were put in place by the project actually worked. You may also be required to identify any new risks and recommend an appropriate strategy to handle them.

Remember that the key to accomplishing this work lies in the understanding of the risk management plan we explained earlier. The plan helps you understand the client's risk attitude and acceptable strategies. The general rule is that for risks that are known and controllable, the response is to deal with the causes. However, for risks that are known but are uncontrollable, the strategy is to deal with the effects.

164

We present here below the various risk management strategies and examples of response plans under each strategy. For a more comprehensive discussion of these, refer to the *PMBOK® Guide* (2013) and Tom (2003).

(i) Risk Avoidance

Risk avoidance is the most effective way to deal with the causes of risks, because it does away with them. However, risk avoidance is not possible for all project risks, because many risks are tightly within the requirements of technical projects. Avoiding risks in your project requires you to reconsider choices and decisions you made in defining and planning your project. Strategies such as buy instead of make, using only tried technology instead of bleeding edge technology etc are examples of risk avoidance.

To avoid schedule risks, reduce the number of critical paths, have fewer activity dependencies, schedule the highest uncertainty activities as early as possible, decompose lengthy activities further and use Critical Chain scheduling techniques. Critical Chain scheduling is also the best approach to managing resource risks. At times when you realize there is too much competition or you do not have a competitive advantage in carrying out some project, you may decide not to compete and cancel the project as a way of avoiding inherent risks.

(ii) Risk Mitigation/ Control/ Reduction

For risks that are intrinsic to your project, avoidance cannot effectively deal with them. Mitigation strategies also called control or reduction strategies reduce the probability or impact of a potential problem. Strategies such as having in place good communication, use of specialists and generalists, strong sponsorship, continued user involvement and clear decision priorities, can be used to reduce the probability and/or impact of a risk occurring.

In a restructuring project where staff have no experience working on restructuring

165

projects, you could contract a structuring specialist to take an assurance role in the project, and provide advice to the Project Board and Project Manager or you could hire experienced restructuring contractors to assist the project staff throughout the project. Other risk reduction strategies could involve bringing the target date of the project forward by paralleling of fast tracking activities so that you bring the project products to the market earlier than competitors.

(iii)Risk Transference

Risk transference involves passing the risks to another party. Passing risk to another party almost always results in paying a premium for this exemption. Risk transference involves some financial implication to be suffered by the third party. The use of fixed price contracts is a classic example of transferring risk from an owner to a contractor. The contractor will bear any cost overrun resulting from implementation of such contracts.

Before deciding to transfer risk the owner should decide which party could best control activities that would lead to the risk occurring and whether the contractor is capable of absorbing the risk. Another way to transfer risk is insurance. Other projects use subcontracting or outsourcing to transfer risks to third parties. The use of bid bonds, performance bonds, retention bonds, warranties and guarantees are other financial instruments used to transfer risks. Yet some projects include a clause in the contract with the selected external supplier stating that, if the full functionality of the project products is not delivered, the selected external supplier will reduce their fees accordingly.

(iv) Exploitation

This strategy may be selected for risks with positive impacts when the organization wishes to ensure that the opportunity is realized. This strategy seeks to eliminate the uncertainty associated with a particular upside risk by making the opportunity definitely happen. Directly exploiting responses include assigning more talented resources to the project to reduce the time to completion, or to provide better quality than originally planned.

(v) Enhancement

This strategy modifies the extent of an opportunity by increasing probability and/or positive impacts, and by identifying and maximizing key drivers of these positive-impacts risks.

Enhancement involves seeking to facilitate or strengthen the cause of the opportunity, and proactively targeting and reinforcing its trigger conditions, might increase probability. Impact drivers can also be targeted, seeking to increase the project's susceptibility to the opportunity.

(vi) Risk Sharing

Risk sharing is a strategy to deal with both threats and opportunities. The strategy allocates proportions of risk to different parties as in the case of the Airbus A300B where research and development risks were allocated among European countries including Britain and France. Risk sharing is appropriate in situations where the threat or opportunity is so large that one party may not handle it alone.

In the banking sector, a borrower may want to acquire funding ranging in billions of US dollars. One lender may not be able to provide all the required amount given the level of exposure to the risk of non repayment or due to the regulations of the banking sector. Such a lender may partner with other lenders to raise the required amount and share with them all the opportunities and threats. This is called syndicate lending and is a form of risk sharing.

Joint ventures, consortia and alliances are also examples of risk sharing. Depending on their structuring, Private Public Partnership could also qualify to be a risk sharing strategy.

(i)   Retaining Risk or Acceptance

This is also called risk assumption strategy. This strategy is adopted because it is seldom possible to eliminate all risks from a project. It may also be adopted when there is no other identifiable risk response strategy. It may be adopted for either threats or opportunities. This strategy can be either passive or active. Passive acceptance requires no action, leaving the project team to deal with the threats or opportunities as they occur.

A passive acceptance strategy could involve relying on the selected external supplier to act in a reliable and conscientious manner to provide the support and advice that will protect the project's interests or recording the risk in the Risk Register and monitoring the situation. Where a competitor is likely to release a particular product before us, we may just carry on with the project as planned on the basis that our product is believed to be of better quality.

Active acceptance is also called fallback strategy and involves putting in place measures to counter the impact of the risk should it occur. The most common active acceptance strategy is to establish a contingency reserve, including amounts of time, money, or resources to handle known – or even sometimes potential, unknown – threats or opportunities. Other examples of active acceptance include requesting for assistance from senior management if difficulties arise in understanding what is happening. Where a project is threatened that a competitor might deliver their project's products earlier, active acceptance of such a risk may involve waiting for confirmation of the rival's products and, if required, include additional gifts with the project's products as an extra incentive.

An example of the risk response plan for critical risks based on the risks listed in Table 17.7 on HIV/AIDS project is shown below:

RISK ID	RISK DESCRIPTION	RECOMMENDED STRATEGY	RISK RESPONSE PLAN
A1	Under-achievement of targets	Risk Control/Mitigation	Involve project Coordinators, M&E and Field officers in routine performance audits of Project Sub Implementers (PSIs) activities so that they can identify and arrest this risk early.
A2	Over-achievement of targets	Risk Enhancement	Most of the PSIs over-achieving targets are coded as Gold. Increase funding limits for these PSIs.
A4	Late submission of reports	Risk control/Mitigation	The Financial Management Agency (FMA) should emphasize timely submission of reports during induction training to PSIs. The field officers and other devolved structures should enforce timely submission of reports
A5	Non documentation	Risk Control/Mitigation	The FMA induction course to PSIs should emphasize the need for documenting PSI transactions for purposes of accountability and transparency. The M&E and Field officers should conduct periodic checks on PSIs to ensure proper documents are kept.
B1	Delayed disbursement of funds	Risk Avoidance	The FMA and Project Advisory Committee should review the current disbursement process to shorten the delays in disbursement to the PSIs, as delayed funding has an impact on the PSI performance
C1	Non completion of projects	Risk Avoidance	Increase monitoring and supervision to identify and manage triggers for the risk of non-completion of projects. The field offices should be more involved as currently helpful here.
C2	Non achievement of objectives	Risk Reduction	Empower the Field Office to use officers under it (such as CACCs, DDOs, regional M&E staff) to conduct Performance Audit(PA) on sub-projects in order to detect in advance the risk of non-achievement of project objectives.
C3	Inability to attract extra funding from other sources	Risk Reduction	FMA can be used to advise the PSIs on extra funding sources
D3	Misappropriation of funds	Risk Avoidance	Discontinue funding for PSIs involved in fraudulent activities and commence recovery. This is the responsibility of head office with advice from the PA, decentralized structures and FMA.
D4	Forgery of project documentation	Risk Avoidance	Discontinue funding for PSIs involved in fraudulent activities and commence recovery. This is the responsibility of head office with advice from the PA, decentralized structures and FMA.
D5	Noninvolvement of PSI officials	Risk Reduction	There should be commitment from the PSI officials that they will be involved in the implementation of the project. Many of such projects have had problems with reporting and compliance because those conducting implementation have not undergone training by the FMA.

Table 17.7: HIV/AIDS Project Risk Response Plan

17.6 Summary

We have now come to the end of this lecture. In this lecture, we explained the difference between qualitative and quantitative risk evaluation. Following that differentiation we discussed how qualitative and quantitative risk assessments are conducted and presented illustrations based on real evaluation.

17.7 Self-test

Using an example of an ongoing project in your organization/context or host institution, trace the planning for risk management for that project. In particular, check whether there is a risk management plan for that project. If it exists, check for its completeness. If it does not exist, reconstruct it. (Remember this can be done as a major project for your host institution).

17.8 Suggestions for further reading

Bruce, T.B. (2005). *Project Risk Management*. Tata McGraw Hill Edition, New Delhi.

Clifford, F.G., & Erick, W.L. (2003), *Project Management: The Managerial Process* (2nd Edition). McGraw Hill.

Kerzner, H. (2008), *Project Management-A Systems Approach to Planning, Scheduling, and Controlling*(10th Edition). John Wiley & Sons Inc.

Project Management Institute, (2013), *A Guide to the Project Management Body of Knowledge,*(5th ed.)Newton Square, PA: Author

Project Management Institute, (2009), *Practice Standard for Project Risk Management*, Newton Square, PA: Author

Tom, K. (2003).*Identifying and Managing Project Risk. Essential Tools for Failure-proofing your project*. AMACOM, New York.

Wideman, R.M. (1992). *Project & Program Risk Management: A guide to managing project risks and opportunities*. Project Management Institute, Newton Square, PA.

LECTUREEIGHTEEN: MONITORING AND EVALUATING TYPOLOGICAL RISK I

Lecture Outline

18.1 Introduction

18.2 Lecture Objectives

18.3The project typology

18.4 Risk, uncertainty and issues

18.5 Techniques of evaluating project uncertainty

18.6 Summary

18.7 Self-test

18.8References and suggestions for further reading

18.1 Introduction

This lecture concerns monitoring and evaluating project contextual risk. The main aspects of project success namely operational excellence, strategic focus and inspired leadership cannot be realized without ensuring that the context in which the project is implemented is enabling proper delivery. The project context is necessarily the environment in which the project is implemented. This environment is characterized by two key dimensions namely uncertainty and complexity. This lecture introduces you to these two dimensions while focusing more on the dimension of uncertainty.

18.2 Lecture Objectives

1. Introduce the concept of project typology
2. Define typological risk
3. Explain the element of uncertainty as a typological risk dimension
4. Present the various approaches to evaluating uncertainty inherent in projects

18.3 Project Typology

An important concept that must be understood by those involved in Monitoring and Evaluation is that of Project Typology, sometimes called Project Environment or Context. Project Typology shows the relationship that exists between the critical elements of complexity and uncertainty. Project complexity is defined in terms of size, value, activities and their interdependence and the number of people or stakeholders involved in the project. Uncertainty on the other hand relates to the likelihood of achieving the project objectives of cost, time, quality, benefits and scope. Different projects exhibit differing typological characteristics as shown in the figure below:

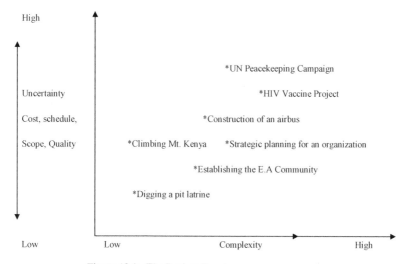

Figure 18.1: The Project Typology

In Fig. 18.1 above, it is shown that a project involving digging a pit latrine has relatively low complexity and low uncertainty. Planning, implementation, monitoring and controlling such a project is relatively easy as the critical dimensions of cost, schedule, scope and performance can be estimated with great certainty at the beginning of the project. On the other hand, a project such as a UN Peace Keeping Campaign is highly complex and highly uncertain. Such a project involves so many stakeholders with

174

contending interests, many interrelated tasks and the critical dimensions of cost, quality and time cannot be estimated accurately since its scope progressively elaborates as the project is implemented. For such projects, methodologies such as PRINCE2[R] and Agile that allow project management by stages are best suited. Using such methodologies, the current stage is planned in great detail with the knowledge of the performance of the previous stages. Stages far away in the cycle are provided for as task packages. These methodologies are a special application of Rolling Wave Planning. Controlling such projects is no mean task! Because their environment is stochastic, and given that these projects typically have multi-million dollar budgets, they require adaptive control with their organization including such layers as corporate or program management, project board, project manager, project team, project support and project assurance.

 What is Rolling Wave Planning? How similar it to Agile Planning?

To the Monitoring and Evaluation (M&E) practitioner, project typology helps to give a rational presentation of the vast range of under-takings where project management principles can be applied. It also gives a clue to the nature of the projects and the difficulties of managing them. Uncertainty particularly affects project planning and complexity particularly affects project control. Project typology gives an indication of the experience and expertise required of the project team. It also indicates the level of seriousness required by the organization executing a given project. Thus, the extent of planning for implementation, monitoring and control of a project becomes more involving as we transition from low-low to high-high typology projects. There are bound to be many more exceptions and variations to the project metrics as we go through this transition.

The M&E effort is also considerably affected by the typology of the project. Consider for example the amount of time and money you will incur in monitoring and evaluating the construction of the multibillion dollar standard gauge railway from the port of Mombasa to Nairobi in Kenya. Compare this with the time and money you will incur in monitoring and evaluation of the implementation of a medium term strategic plan of an organization.

From this discussion, it can be concluded that project typology is a major source of project risk and thus it shapes the recommendations that you can make in view of monitoring and evaluation that has been done. Typological risk is a function of two critical project elements namely; uncertainty and complexity. Uncertainty is considered in depth in Management Science texts and complexity is also handled in depth in the PMI (2014) Practice Guide on Navigating Complexity.

Working in groups explain the implication of high typological risk on project communication.

18.4 Risk, Uncertainty and Issues

Recall that we defined risk as the effect of uncertainty on project objectives. Uncertainty refers to a state of imperfect knowledge about a future event. Risks and uncertainties are distinguishable from issues. An issue is something that has happened and either threatens or enhances the success of the project. Risks and uncertainties are things that might happen. When a risky or an uncertain event occurs on the project, it becomes an issue implying that an issue occurs either as a result of an identified risk or uncertain event occurring. When an issue occurs, it can either be dealt with within the project as defined or will require change in order to keep the project viable.

PRINCE2[R] uses the term issue to cover any relevant event that has happened, was not planned, and requires management action. The PRINCE2[R] (2009) manual on *Managing Successful Projects with PRINCE2[TM]* classifies issues into three: request for change, off specification and problem or concern.

Explain with examples what is meant by:
a) Request for Change
b) Off-specification
c) Problem/concern

Generally, when an issue is identified on a project, record it in the issues log and then decide and agree on how it will be resolved including determining who will be in charge of its resolution. Once the issue has been resolved, record the date and method of resolution in the issues log. Where the issue requires changes to the critical dimensions of the project then it should be handled within the integrated change management system of the project. All significant issues should be reported and discussed in progress review meetings.

In a risk environment, we can assign probabilities to events and therefore we are able to determine the expected values. Under uncertainty, we may not able to assign probabilities to the events because they are unknown-unknowns. Notice that risks are known-unknowns. Like is the case with risk, decision making under uncertainty acknowledges that there is no dominant strategy.

18.5 Techniques of evaluating project uncertainty
Recall that we have used the word uncertainty to mean the inability to accurately estimate cost, scope, quality, benefits and timescale for a given project owing to lack of perfect knowledge about these dimensions. In an environment characterized by high uncertainty, say during hyperinflationary or stag-flationary times, it is rarely possible to estimate the

project accurately. Project estimation in such environment requires use of more advanced techniques. Kerzner (2008) documents these techniques as follows:

Hurwicz Criterion: This is also referred to as the Maximax criterion. Under this criterion, the decision maker is always optimistic and always wants to maximize outcome. In determining the decision to take under the Hurwicz criterion, we consider only the maximum payoffs under each strategy and then choose the strategy with the greatest value. Sometimes the payoffs under this criterion are scaled down by a coefficient of optimism which shows the degree to which the decision maker is optimistic that the payoffs will be realized.

Maximin Criterion: This is also called the Wald criterion. Here the decision maker is concerned with how much he or she can afford to lose. Thus this criterion is the opposite of the Hurwicz criterion. The decision maker is rather pessimistic as opposed to the Maximax criterion in which the decision maker was optimistic. The idea here is to minimize the maximum loss by considering only the minimum payoffs for each strategy and then choosing that strategy with the least value of the loss. The payoffs under this criterion can also be scaled down by a coefficient of pessimism to depict the extent to which a decision maker is optimistic.

Minimax Criterion: This is also called the Savage criterion. The decision maker is concerned with minimizing regrets by choosing among several strategies. To do this, we begin by setting up a regrets table. This is done by subtracting all payoffs for each strategy from the largest payoff for that strategy. This gives values called regrets. The maximum regret is the largest regret for each strategy. The decision maker then selects a strategy that yields the minimum of these maximum regrets.

Laplace Criterion: This is also called the Equally likely criterion. This criterion attempts to transform decision making under uncertainty to decision making under risk. According to this criterion, if the probabilities of each state of nature are not known then we can assume that each state of nature has equal likelihood of occurrence. So each state of nature is assigned equal probability

178

and the expected value (EV) of each strategy is calculated. The strategy with the highest EV or the minimum expected loss is then chosen.

Use the case illustration provided in class to advise the organization you work for on which course of action should be taken under each of the above uncertainty evaluation criteria.

18.6 Summary

We have now come to the end of this lecture. In this lecture, we defined the concept of project typology and its components. We also explained what is meant by typological risk and discussed how one of its components-uncertainty is evaluated.

18.7 Self-test
Based on your experience from your context/organization/host institution, how is the element of uncertainty modeled into projects?

18.8 References and suggestions for further reading

AXELOS Ltd.-OGC. (2009). *Managing Successful Projects with PRINCE2™*. The Stationery Office, UK.

Kerzner, H. (2008), *Project Management-A Systems Approach to Planning, Scheduling, and Controlling* (10th Edition). John Wiley & Sons Inc.

Project Management Institute (2009). *Practice Standard for Project Risk Management*, Newton Square, PA: Author.

Wideman, R.M. (1992). *Project & Program Risk Management: A guide to managing project risks and opportunities*. Project Management Institute, Newton Square, PA.

Taylor, B.W. (2002). *Introduction to Management Science* (7th Edition).Prentice Hall. New Jersey.

LECTURE NINETEEN: MONITORING AND EVALUATING TYPOLOGICAL RISK II
Lecture Outline

19.1 Introduction

19.2 Lecture Objectives

19.3 Introduction to complexity theory

19.4 Explain the operation of complexity theory

19.5 Categories of project complexity

19.5.1 Human behavior

19.5.2 System behavior

19.5.3 Ambiguity

19.6 Summary

19.7 Self-test

19.8 Suggestions for further reading

19.1 Introduction
This lecture introduces the other aspect of typology, namely the element of complexity. Recall that we defined complexity in the previous lecture to comprise the number of activities on the project and their interdependence, the number of stakeholders on the project and the variety of cultures on the project. This lecture is meant to show how complexity can be broken down on a project and how the risk brought about by complex systems on the project can be monitored and evaluated.

19.2 Lecture Objectives
1. Introduce the arguments of complexity theory
2. Identify the main components of complexity to be monitored and evaluated
3. Discuss the implication of complexity theory to project control
4. Explain how project complexity enhances typological risk

19.3 Introduction to Complexity Theory

A major aspect of project typology is the element of complexity. The argument of project complexity is drawn from *complexity theory* which states that critically interacting components self-organize to form potentially evolving structures exhibiting a hierarchy of emergent system properties (Lucas 2009). This theory takes the view that systems are best regarded as wholes, and studied as such, rejecting the traditional emphasis on simplification and reduction as inadequate techniques on which to base this sort of scientific work. Such techniques, whilst valuable in investigation and data collection, fail in their application at system level due to the inherent nonlinearity of strongly interconnected systems - the causes and effects are not separate and the whole is not the sum of the parts.

There is a close link between complexity theory and the *theory of chaos. Chaos theory* is a field of study in mathematics, with applications in several disciplines including Project Management. Chaos theory studies the behavior of dynamical systems that are highly sensitive to initial conditions—a response popularly referred to as the butterfly effect. Small differences in initial conditions (such as those due to rounding errors in numerical computation) yield widely diverging outcomes for such dynamical systems, rendering long-term prediction impossible in general (Kellert 1993). This happens even though these systems are deterministic, meaning that their future behavior is fully determined by their initial conditions, with no random elements involved. In other words, the deterministic nature of these systems does not make them predictable (Werndl 2009). The chaos theory was summarized by Lorenz (1963) as follows:

"Chaos: When the present determines the future, but the approximate present does not approximately determine the future".

 What in your opinion is the main difference between *chaos* and *complexity*?

While complexity theory is strikingly similar to chaos theory, complexity theorists maintain that chaos, by itself, does not account for the coherence of self-organizing, complex systems. Rather, complex systems reside at the edge of chaos-the actors or components of a system are never locked in to a particular position or role within the system, but they never fall completely out of control. In Complexity, the edge of chaos is the constantly shifting battle zone between stagnation and anarchy (*order and disorder*), the one place where a complex system can be spontaneous, adaptive, and alive.

However, it has since been established that complexity theory emerged from chaos theory (Mitchell M. W.1993) with complexity being the midpoint between order and disorder.

19.4 The Operation of Complexity Theory

According to the PMI Practice Guide on Navigating Complexity (2014), a complex system is defined as one in which many independent agents interact with each other in multiple (sometimes infinite) ways. This variety of actors also allows for the spontaneous self-organization that sometimes takes place in a system. This self-organization occurs without anyone being in charge or planning the organization. Rather, it is more a result of organisms/agents constantly adapting to each other. The complex systems are also adaptive (i.e., they always adapt in a way that benefits them) in a manner similar to the way the human brain adapts to learn from experience (Battram, 2002).

Another important concept in complexity theory is that there is no master controller of any system. Rather, coherent system behavior is generated by the competition and cooperation between actors that is always present. The components of a system have different levels of organization-made up of divisions, which contain different departments, which in turn comprise different workers. But the important differentiation from this organization is that complex adaptive systems are constantly revising and rearranging their building blocks as they gain experience. A firm will promote individuals who do well and (more rarely) will reshuffle its organizational chart for greater efficiency. Countries will make new trading agreements or realign themselves into whole new alliances (Caldart & Joan, 2004).

According to Olsen, Glenda, Richard &Peter (2001), complexity theory assumes that there are principles underlying all emergent properties, or traits that emerge from the interactions of many different actors. One of the defining characteristics of complex systems is the inability to predict the outcome of any given change to the system. Because a system depends on so many intricate interactions, the number of possible reactions to any given change is infinite. Minor events can have enormous consequences because of the chain of reactions they might incite.

Conversely, major changes may have an almost insignificant effect on the system as a whole. Because of this, strong control of any complex system may be impossible. While it may have order, no one absolutely governs a complex system. Scientists create computer simulations that enable them to better identify emerging patterns in a system. They also write modification programs allowing system components to adapt to changes in the environment without the absolute necessity of radical changes to the overall structure. Computers can use these simulations to design production schedules and optimize assembly line performance. Howard & Ron (1999) believe business today is faster and nonlinear (effects are not proportional to their causes), and that experts cannot predict which products or companies will succeed. Sherman and Schultz (1998) assert that competitive advantage is fleeting, and that change can rapidly turn assets into dead weight.

What in your opinion are the differences between project life cycle theory and complexity theory?

19.5 Implication of Complexity Theory to Projects

In the previous lecture we presented the element of complexity to be the second determinant of the project's typological risk. We defined complexity to comprise the number of tasks to be performed on the project, the degree of interrelatedness among these tasks, the number of stakeholders on the project, the communication channels on the project and the number of cultures represented on the project. In some contexts, uncertainty is taken to be part of complexity. For example, as we will see shortly, the PMI Practice Guide on Navigating Complexity classifies uncertainty as an aspect of complexity. Because of its central role in shaping the nature and extent of monitoring and evaluation, we will consider the element of complexity in great depth.

According to the PMI Practice Guide on Navigating Complexity (2014), programs and projects with complexity may fluctuate between conditions of relative stability and predictability to instability and uncertainty. The organization's prior experience, talent management and effective communications will often influence the perception of complexity and its influence on the program or project. Generally, project complexity is divided into three categories namely *human behavior, ambiguity* and *systems behavior.* We present here below a brief explanation of each of these categories. For a comprehensive discussion of these categories, refer to the PMI (2014) *Navigating Complexity: A Practice Guide.*

19.5.1 Human Behavior

Human behavior is a key determinant of ineffective project control. Stakeholders may set unrealistic expectations or may continue shifting their expectations on the project by making uncontrolled scope changes to the project design. Human behavior can also manifest itself in the various cultural orientations of the key stakeholders-some cultures may be supportive of project delivery while others may not. Different cultures may also favor different modes of communication. The level of organizational maturity, development and design may also influence the extent of project complexity. Misalignment of the project with the organization's goals can make project delivery a very complex process since senior management may not see the need of committing resources to such a project.

Opacity-the way in which an organization conducts its business i.e. makes decisions, determines strategies and sets priorities may also affect the perception of stakeholders towards the organization's projects thus affecting their degree of complexity and control. Teams with tribal mindset, groupthink and the existence of group shift can also make a project become more complex. At times, people self-organize themselves in ways that may not be supportive of project delivery. Another human behavior related cause of complexity is the lack of stakeholder commitment to the cause of the project.

19.5.2 Ambiguity
Ambiguity is a state of being unclear about what to expect from a situation. Ambiguity arises from unclear or misleading events, cause and effect confusion, emergent issues or even from situations open to more than one interpretation on the project. With this understanding, uncertainty can be seen as an aspect of ambiguity and thus complexity. Emergence of unanticipated change that occurs within the context of a program or project may cause complexity in the project. Sometimes delivery of the first project phase may lead to results that may require redesigning the entire project.

19.5.3 System Behavior
Relationships existing between the various components of a project or program such as the interrelatedness among project tasks can create complexity within a project or program. Complexity increases with the number of connections. For example, the number of communication channels (C) increase with the number of stakeholders (N) according to the formula $C = N\left(\dfrac{N-1}{2}\right)$. Also when project design is not done well so that there are a number of missing components, complexity is likely to increase. Dependencies among project components also cause complexity. When work packages are interdependent, a delay in the delivery of one work package causes a delay across

the project. Dependencies between the project and its environment and between the program and project may also cause complexity. When both connectedness and interdependency of components exist together so as to cause change over time, what results is referred to as system dynamics. The interactions among components of the system may cause interconnected risks, draw on resources and create emerging unforeseen issues. An example of system dynamics may be replacing a competent project manager with someone who does not possess the required competencies or has totally different qualities and skills.

19.6 Summary

We have now come to the end of this lecture. In this lecture, we introduced complexity theory and discussed its operation and implications to project management. We also presented the categories of project complexity with clear identification of what aspects contribute to complexity and thus typological risk.

 19.7 Self-test

Suppose that your host institution has asked you to evaluate the extent of typological risk due to complexity within their projects. Develop a checklist that you will use to accomplish this task.

19.8 Suggestions for further reading

Battram, A., (2002). *Navigating Complexity: The Essential Guide to Complexity Theory in Business and Management.* London: Spiro Press.

Caldart, A. A., & Joan, E. R., (2004)."*Corporate Strategy Revisited: A View from Complexity Theory.*"European Management Review 1, no. 1.

Howard S. & Ron, S. (1999). *Open Boundaries: Creating Business Innovation Through Complexity.* John Wiley.

Kellert, S. H., (1993). *In the Wake of Chaos: Unpredictable Order in Dynamical Systems.* University of Chicago Press.p. 32.

Lorenz, Edward N. (1963). "*Deterministic non-periodic flow*". Journal of the Atmospheric Sciences 20 (2): 130–141.

Lucas (2009).*Quantifying complexity.*www.calresco.org/lucas/quantify.htm

Mitchell, M. W. (1993). *Complexity: The Emerging Science at the Edge of Order and Chaos.* John Wiley

Olsen, E. E., Glenda H. E., Richard, B., & Peter, V. (2001).*Facilitating Organization Change: Lessons from Complexity Science.* San Francisco: Pfeiffer, 2001.

Project Management Institute (2014). *Navigating Complexity: A Practice Guide.* Newton Square, PA: Author

Sherman, H.J., and Ralph S., (1998).*Open Boundaries: Creating Business Innovation Through Complexity.* Reading, MA: Perseus Books

Werndl, C., (2009). "*What are the New Implications of Chaos for Unpredictability?*" The British Journal for the Philosophy of Science 60 (1): 195–220.

LECTURE TWENTY: HANDLING TYPOLOGICAL RISK
Lecture Outline

20.1 Introduction

20.2 Lecture Objectives

20.3 Scope and Time Management under risk

20.4 Human Resources and Communication Management under risk

20.5 PRINCE2[R] Methodology

20.6 Summary

20.7 Self-test

20.8 Suggestions for further reading

20.1 Introduction
Planning and managing projects under conditions of complexity and uncertainty is generally more demanding than if it was the case of a project implemented in a deterministic and linear environment. Monitoring and evaluation practitioners should clearly understand the kind of recommendations they ought to make under risk.

20.2 Lecture Objectives

1. Explain how scope and time should be handled under risk

2. Explain how human resource management and communication should be handled under risk

3. Explain how integration management should be handled under risk

4. Introduce the principles of PRINCE2[R] Methodology

5. Identify alternative strategies to recommend following project monitoring and evaluation

---

20.3 Scope and Time Management under risk

Handling project complexity (and uncertainty) requires careful analysis for the causes of that complexity (and uncertainty). Ambiguity generally affects the process of scope definition and control. Recall from your training in Project Management that scope definition is the basis of developing scope, schedule and cost baselines. In an ambiguous typology, developing these baselines can prove to be very difficult. In such cases:

- Ensure proper use of integrated change control,
- Use flexible, adaptive and iterative life cycles,
- Use rolling wave/agile planning and progressive elaboration,
- Undertake proper requirements planning with clear traceability matrices,
- Break down work to ensure all work packages are identified
- Use Critical Chain Management approach to schedule projects

In a guided discussion session, discuss the appropriateness of each of these recommended approaches to handle scope and time under risk

20.4 Human Resources and Communication Management under risk

Human and system behavior generally affect project estimation in the sense that they are likely to lead to optimism bias-the tendency of human beings to think that they are less likely to make errors than others. Optimism bias is classified as one of the main causes of unsuccessful projects as it leads to underestimation of project cost and time while overestimating project benefits. The use of reference class forecasting is usually encouraged to counter the effects of optimism bias. Engaging in pre-mortem reviews (risk pre-assessments) and external audits of the estimates and other project metrics can also help reduce and control typological risk.

190

Explain how you will structure communication on a complex project

20.5 PRINCE2® Methodology

Adoption of the PRINCE2® methodology provides a structured way of dealing with the typological risk on the projects. The application of the seven PRINCE2® principles in managing complex and uncertain projects enhances PDC by reducing the impact of the inherent typological risk. We briefly introduce each of these principles below:

Continued Business Justification:

We did emphasize earlier that every project must have a business case and that this business case must continue to exist throughout the life cycle of the project. Just in case the business case is lost mid stream, the project should be discontinued. This ensures that the project remains aligned to the business objectives, strategy and benefits being sought.

The executive role on the project board is meant to ensure the continued business justification. The aspects of complexity discussed earlier i.e. human behavior, ambiguity and system dynamics can interact to distort the business case of the project and so in order to control the impact of such distortion, PRINCE2® recommends continued business justification during starting up a project, at project initiation and at the end of every consequent stage.

Manage by Stages:

In a bid to break down project complexity to manageable levels and as planning can only be done to a level that is manageable and foreseeable, PRINCE2® recommends that projects are planned, monitored and controlled on a stage-by-stage basis, providing control points at major intervals throughout the project. This is important since the scope of the project elaborates progressively as the project is implemented. Managing by stages ensures that the current phase is planned in detail using the experience gained from the previous stage(s).Work to be performed later is provided for as task packages.

191

Learn from ***Experience:***	At/close to the end of, every management stage, PRINCE2[R] recommends that the project manager completes end stage reports and also updates the lessons learned log with any lessons regarding what worked and what didn't. These lessons are used to inform planning for the next work pages in the following stages. This ensures that the project proactively addresses any deviations in expected human and systems behavior in time and also addresses any emerging ambiguity within the project.
Defined Roles ***and*** ***Responsibilities:***	PRINCE2[R] recommends a project structure with key roles and responsibilities. Some of these roles include corporate or program management, project board, project manager, team manager, project support and project assurance. Corporate/program management give the project mandate. The board is in charge of the delivery of the overall project and ensures user, supplier and business interests of the project and approves any exceptions that are within their tolerances. Involvement of the corporate/program management and the board in the project ensures that the project is aligned to the strategic objectives of the organization and benefits from top management support. The board provides a key governance mechanism for the project and advises and directs the project manager as required.
Manage by ***Exception:***	PRINCE2[R] projects establish distinct limits of authority for each level of the project management team, based on the performance objectives of time, cost, scope (the classic triple constraints) adding in quality, risk and benefits to provide a full and truer picture of a project's success factors. Each authority level has clear tolerances allocated to it and where such tolerances are set to be exceeded, this is escalated to next authority level.

The board delegates the day-to-day management of the project to the project manager with agreed tolerances. Where these tolerances are set to be exceeded, the project manager must escalate this to the board. The board reviews the sought exception and either approves or declines.

Focus on Products:	We stated earlier that ambiguity affects project scope definition so that developing a work break down structure for the entire project becomes difficult. To handle this, PRINCE2® recommends breaking down a project by products and project planning focuses on these products. Thus at scope definition level, a project product description is developed and on the basis of this a product break down structure for each product is developed. Work break down structures are developed by team managers following negotiated work packages with the project manager. This way, the effect of ambiguity on scope definition is controlled.
Tailor to Suit the Project Environment:	Every project is unique. This uniqueness is characterized by the uncertainty and complexity (typological risk) inherent in the project. Thus, project management practices must be tailored to recognize the environment in which the project is being implemented in order to avoid robotic project management. This way, the project is designed in such a way that the impact of the typological risk on its objectives is controlled.

Explain how project control is optimized by applying PRINCE2® Methodology

20.6 Other ways of handling typological risks

Other ways of handling typological risk include:

- Having in place a clear and functional communication strategy
- Having in place a clear and functional stakeholder engagement plan
- Having in place a risk management strategy
- Ensuring that the organizational structure chosen is optimal and appropriate
- Establish effective project governance
- Use experienced and appropriate teams
- Manage project integration effectively
- Establish an early warning system on the project
- Ensure that a project kick off meeting is conducted and attended by all key stakeholders

20.7 Strategies to pursue following Project Performance Assessment

Once a project assessment has been undertaken, project management can pursue any of the following strategies particularly where performance is not to the expected levels:

- Renegotiation- discuss with your client the prospect of increasing the budget for the project or extending the deadline for completion.
- Recover during later steps if you begin to fall behind in early steps of a project, re-examine budgets and schedule for later steps
- Narrow project scope – perhaps non-essential elements of the project can be eliminated reducing time and cost
- Deploy more resources – more people or machines to be able to meet planned targets in cost and time
- Accept substitution when inputs are not available or are more expensive but this should not compromise on quality.
- Seek alternative sources – when suppliers cannot deliver within budget or schedule.

- Accept partial delivery – sometimes suppliers cannot deliver all that is required on schedule. In this case, you can recommend partial delivery.
- Offer incentives – may require going beyond the original budget of the contract to encourage on time delivery.
- Demand compliance – that people deliver results as agreed. This happens where the project is fixed in cost, time or quality.

20.8 Summary

We have now come to the end of this lecture. In this lecture, we explained how to deal with typological risk focusing on the elements of time, scope, human resources and communication. We also briefly introduced the principles of the PRINCE2[R] methodology that are key in managing constrained projects. Finally, we have presented several strategies that may be pursued following monitoring and evaluation

20.9 Self-test

In the face of constraints, some projects turn to the use of critical chain project management methodology which follows Goldratt's theory of constraints. You were introduced to this methodology during your study of project management. Explain how this methodology handles typological risk.

20.10 Suggestions for further reading

AXELOS Ltd.-OGC. (2009). *Managing Successful Projects with PRINCE2™.*The Stationery Office, UK.
Project Management Institute (2014). *Navigating Complexity: A Practice Guide.* Newton Square, PA: Author
Kerzner, H. (2008). *Project Management-A Systems Approach to Planning, Scheduling, and Controlling* (10th Edition).John Wiley & Sons Inc.

LECTURE TWENTY-ONE: EVALUATING STAKEHOLDER RISK
Lecture Outline

21.1 Introduction
This lecture introduces the subject of stakeholder risk. Stakeholders are the main source of ineffective control on projects. They contribute enormously to typological risk and their management is crucial for project delivery. Notice that the project benefits, products, results and services accrue to the stakeholder and if stakeholder risk is not adequately determined and dealt with, delivery of these benefits may be illusionary.

21.2 Lecture Objectives

1. Explain the concept of participatory monitoring and evaluation

2. Discuss the processes involved in stakeholder management

3. Distinguish between the concept of managing stakeholders on projects and managing projects for stakeholders

21.3 Rationale for stakeholder participation

Involving stakeholders in project monitoring and evaluation has been generally referred to as Participatory Monitoring & Evaluation (PM&E). PM&E is the collective examination and assessment of a program or project by the stakeholders and beneficiaries. This approach to M&E is hailed as being reflective, action-oriented and seeks to build capacity among stakeholders. It is primarily oriented to the information needs of the stakeholders rather than the donor who acts as a facilitator. It is about radically rethinking who initiates and undertakes the process of M&E and who learns or benefits from the findings. It involves local people, development agencies and policy makers deciding together how progress should be measured and results acted upon. Using this approach can reveal valuable lessons and improve accountability within an institution or on the project.

Participatory M&E provides an opportunity for development organizations to focus better on their ultimate goal of improving poor people's lives. By broadening involvement in identifying and analyzing change, a clearer picture can be gained of what is really happening on the ground. It allows people to celebrate successes and learn from failures. For those involved, it can also be a very empowering process, since it puts them in charge; helps develop skills and shows that their views count.

When talking about participatory M&E, we are always reminded of the saying that it is the wearer of the shoe who knows where it pinches. If people require slippers but you instead give them shoes, don't be surprised to find them having cut the shoes into slippers at the time of impact assessment! Participatory M&E therefore implies opening up the design of the process to include those most directly affected, and agreeing to analyze data together.

Participatory M&E approaches include the use of oral histories, photos, videos and theatre. Others are:

- Maps: to show the location and types of changes in the area being monitored.

198

- Venn diagrams: to show changes in relationships between groups, institutions, and individuals.
- Flow diagrams: to show direct and indirect impacts of changes, and to relate them to causes.
- Diaries: to describe changes in the lives of individuals or groups.
- Photographs: to depict changes through a sequence of images.
- Matrix scoring: to compare people's preference for a set of options or outcomes.
- Network diagrams: to show changes in the type and degree of contact between people and service.

Using these approaches, stakeholders are able to track changes and impact that is occurring in their contexts as a result of a given intervention. It is emphasized that for these approaches to work well, stakeholders must be encouraged to participate in the project through a clear and transparent engagement strategy. Also there must exist a good baseline against which changes can be benchmarked. Again note that it is important that the stakeholders also participate in generating the baseline data. This way, you can be certainly sure of enhanced PDC, project ownership and sustainability.

21.4 Conducting stakeholders' analysis

Stakeholder analysis involves identifying stakeholders and determining their requirements or interests so that a responsive engagement strategy can be determined. Project stakeholder identification activity is aimed at systematically identifying as many project stakeholders as possible to create a stakeholder register.

This register, created through detailed stakeholder analysis, lists the stakeholders and categorizes their relationship to the program, their ability to influence the program outcome, their degree of support for the program, and other characteristics or attributes the program manager feels could influence the stakeholders' perception and the program's outcome (*PMBOK® Guide*, 2013)

Stakeholder Identification is conducted through the following steps:

199

Step 1: Perform *LePEST/PESTLe* analysis of the project environment.

- The Legal environment (Le) includes regulatory authorities such as the municipal and city councils, government environmental authorities and other licensing organs.

- Political environment (P) includes the political set up including area MPs, county representatives, county governors and even the presidency.

- Economic environment (E) describes suppliers, donors, competitors and buyers or users of the project products/services/results.

- The Social environment (S) includes the religious institutions, community groupings, professional bodies, special interest groups and cultural institutions that could influence the delivery of the project.

- Technological environment (T) describes the owners and suppliers of knowledge and skill required to deliver the project. This includes the project experts, the project management office etc.

Following this approach, we develop an exhaustive list of all the stakeholders involved in the project.

Step 2:   Draw up a stakeholder table that lists the stakeholders identified in step 1 above together with their contacts.

• For each stakeholder identify their interest in the project. For example, a team member's interest in the project can be identified as "income" whereas a shareholder's interest in a project can be identified as "wealth maximization".

• Make an assessment of the likely impact of the project on each interest identified. This is key because stakeholder management is about management of their interests. With this information, now indicate the relative priority that the project should give to addressing each interest.

• This process provides a basis for categorizing stakeholders into say primary or secondary, core or non-core, key or non-key, supporters or opposes etc.

There are various classification models for stakeholder analysis. A commonly used classification is that of *Power Interest Grid* (see the *PMBOK® Guide* (2013) for more classification models. This groups stakeholders based on their level of authority (power) and their level of concern (interest) regarding the project outcomes. A power interest grid may appear as follows:

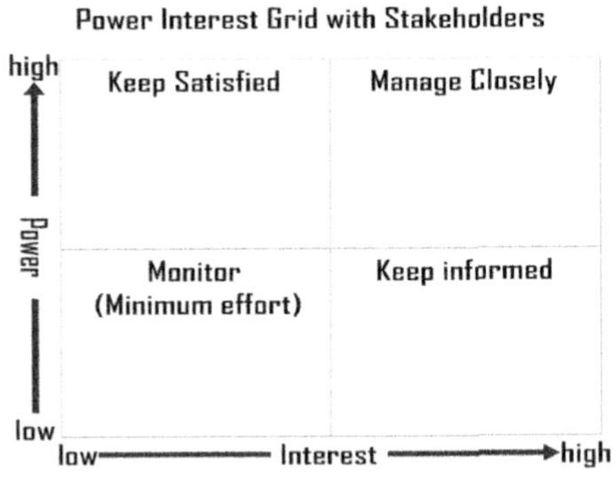

Figure 21.1: Power Interest Grid with Stakeholders

201

Steps (1) and (2) give rise to the stakeholder register. The stakeholder register is the main output of the Identify Stakeholder process. The register contains identification, assessment and stakeholder classification information. Notice that the register does not contain the stakeholder management strategy. Whereas the stakeholder register is a document to be accessed by all, the management strategy contains classified information that is not available to all. The register is updated as the project is implemented to keep track of any changes in the project environment. A stakeholder register lists the names of the stakeholders, their contact information, their role in the project, their project requirements and expectations, their influence on the project and classification.

Step 3: Arising from step (2), draw up a stakeholder participation strategy and discuss with each stakeholder how they will participate in the project. Note that this step is done during the planning of stakeholder engagement.

According to the *PMBOK® Guide* (2013), stakeholder engagement planning activity outlines how all program stakeholders will be engaged throughout the duration of the program. The stakeholder register is analyzed with consideration of the organization's strategic plan, program charter, and program business case to understand the environment in which the program will operate. As a part of the stakeholder analysis and engagement planning, the following aspects for each stakeholder will be considered:

- Organizational culture and acceptance of change
- Attitudes about the program and its sponsors
- Expectation of program benefits delivery
- Degree of support or opposition to the program benefits
- Ability to influence the outcome of the program

This effort results in the stakeholder engagement plan which contains a detailed strategy for effective stakeholder engagement for the duration of the program. The plan includes stakeholder engagement guidelines and provides insight about how the stakeholders of

202

various components of a program are engaged. The plan defines the metrics used to measure the performance of stakeholder engagement activities. This should not only include measures of participation in meetings and other communications channels, but should also strive to measure the effectiveness of the engagement in meeting its intended goal (*PMBOK® Guide*, 2013). The guidelines for project-level stakeholder engagement should be provided to the component projects and non-project work under the program. The stakeholder engagement plan provides critical information used in the development of the program's communications plan and its ongoing alignment as the known stakeholders change. The current engagement levels of all stakeholders need to be compared to the planned engagement levels required for successful project completion. Stakeholder engagement throughout the lifecycle of the project is critical to project success. According to the *PMBOK® Guide* (2013) the engagement levels of stakeholders can be classified as:

- Unaware. Unaware of project and potential impacts
- Resistant. Aware of project and potential impacts and resistant to change
- Neutral. Aware of project yet neither supportive nor resistant
- Supportive. Aware of project and potential impacts and supportive to change
- Leading. Aware of project and potential impacts and actively engaged in ensuring the project is a success

In addition to data gathered in the stakeholder register, the stakeholder management plan often provides:

- Desired and current engagement levels of stakeholders
- Scope and impact of change to stakeholders
- Identified interrelationships and overlaps among stakeholders
- Stakeholder communication requirements
- Information to be distributed to stakeholders including language, format, content, level of detail reason for distribution and timeframe and frequency
- Method for updating and refining the stakeholder management plan

203

21.5 Stakeholder Management Strategy

A stakeholder management strategy documents the stakeholder names, their influence on the project, how the project is likely to impact on their interest and the strategies to be used to manage the stakeholder interests. Typically, there are four forms of participation strategies commonly used on projects. These are:

Information strategy:	This strategy is used for those stakeholders who may not have influence on the impact of the project but somehow must be informed of the project progress. Take an example of an awareness campaign project. You may need to inform the village elder or headsman or even local administration to carry on the awareness campaign. Equally, you may need to inform the police if you are going to host large crowds in the campaign.
Consultation strategy:	We consult with stakeholders who have expert knowledge in the area of the project. If you are drilling boreholes then you may consult with water engineers and geologists. If you are building a commercial building you will consult with planning authorities, architects, construction engineers etc.
Partnering strategy:	We partner with stakeholders who control a resource needed by the project. If you are using labor provided by a union, then you will partner with the union. If you are building a facility on community land, then you will partner with the community. If you are acquiring land by way of purchase from people to put up a facility, don't just be satisfied by the fact that you have paid them money. Consider partnering with them say by way of employment etc. Otherwise they will come back to haunt your project!
	We also partner with project sponsors (they are today called partners not donors!)
Controlling strategy:	Stakeholders with technical expertise in the area of the project such as team members and key primary stakeholders such as senior users, senior suppliers and executives

Illustration

In the example below, Financier Bank Ltd. is installing a financial switch project that will enable it meet its customers' demand for cash efficiently and effectively. Stakeholders have been identified and categorized as shown in the table below:

	Interests	Likely impact of project on interest	Relative Priorities of
Primary stakeholders			
Personal Sector Department	Sales volume Profits	+ +/-	1
Target Customers	Convenient access to funds	+	1
Project Sponsor	Achievement of targets	+	1
Secondary Stakeholders			
Finance Department	Control of funds	-	3
IT Department	Control of IT resources	-	3
Hardware vendors	Sales volume Profits	+ +/-	2
Software vendors	Sales volume Profits	+ +/-	2
Advertising Agency	Profits Public Image	+ +/-	2
Central Bank of Kenya	Regulations	+/-	3
Local Authority	By-laws	+/-	2
Wells Fargo	Profits Public Image	+ +/-	2
Paynet Kenya Ltd.	Profits Public Image	+ +/-	2
Kenya Data Network (KDN)	Profits Public Image	+ +/-	2
Kenya Power & Lighting Co. Ltd.	Profits	+	2
Competitors	Market Share	-	5

Table 21.1: Stakeholder Identification Table

The table below shows a sample stakeholder engagement plan for the Financier Bank Ltd. described above:

Stage in Life	Participation Strategy			
Cycle	Inform (I)	Consult (C)	Partner (P)	Control (C)
Identification & Appraisal		Project Sponsor Target customers	Paynet	
Planning & Financial Approval		Paynet	Paynet Vendors	Project Director
Implementation			Paynet Vendors	Project Director Project Manager Personal Sector Dept.
Monitoring & Evaluation	Project sponsor/ Project Director		Paynet Vendors	Project Director

Table 21.2: Stakeholder participation strategy

 Working in groups, stage a debate session on whether we should manage stakeholders on projects or whether we should manage projects for stakeholders.

21.6 Summary

We have now come to the end of this lecture. In this lecture, we explained the concept of stakeholder and stakeholder management and presented the rationale for stakeholder analysis. We have also discussed the main steps involved in conducting stakeholder analysis on a project. Finally, we have explained the main stakeholder management strategies and debated whether we should manage stakeholders on projects or should manage projects for stakeholders.

21.7 Self-test

Consider a major project that is currently being implemented by your host institution. Trace its planning for stakeholder engagement plan. Does the project have a stakeholder engagement plan? If No, construct this plan for the project.

21.8 Suggestions for further reading

Lousa, G. & Mike, E. (2003).*Toolkits: A practical guide to planning, monitoring, evaluation and impact assessment* (2nd edition). London: Save the Children.

Freeman, R.E., Jeffrey, H., & Andrew, W. (2007).*Managing for Stakeholders.* New Haven: Yale University   Press.

Project Management Institute, (2013).*A Guide to the Project Management Body of Knowledge* (5th ed.). Newton Square, PA: Author

LECTURE TWENTY-TWO: MONITORING AND EVALUATING PROJECT QUALITY

Lecture Outline

22.1 Introduction

22.2 Lecture Objectives

22.3 Rationale for project Quality Monitoring and Evaluation

22.4 An overview of the Quality Movement

22.5 Quality Assurance and Control

22.6 Acceptance Sampling

22.7 Summary

22.8 Self-test

23.9 Suggestions for further Reading

22.1 Introduction

This lecture introduces you to project quality monitoring and evaluation. Recall from the "Iron Triangle" that the key measures of operational excellence on projects are cost, quality and time. Recall again that the word "quality" as used on projects refers to both technical and performance aspects of the project. The focus of this lecture is to provide the framework that is useful in monitoring and evaluating both technical and performance quality on projects.

22.2 Lecture Objectives

| 1. Explain the rationale for monitoring and evaluating project quality |
| 2. Briefly introduce the quality movement |
| 3. Explain the difference between quality assurance and control |
| 4. Discuss the various techniques used in quality assurance and control |
| 5. Understand the need for and practice of acceptance sampling on projects |

22.3 Rationale for Project Quality Monitoring and Evaluation

According to the *PMBOK*[R] *Guide* (2013), project quality management includes the processes and activities of the performing organization that determine quality policies, objectives and responsibilities so that the project will satisfy the needs for which it was undertaken. Project quality management supports continuous process improvement activities as undertaken on behalf of the performing organization. It ensures that project requirements, including product requirements are met and validated.

Quality is the degree to which a set of inherent characteristics fulfill requirements. This is distinguished from a grade which is a category assigned to deliverables having the same functional use but different technical characteristics. While a quality level that fails to meet quality requirements is always a problem, a low grade of quality may not be a problem.

Modern quality management generally recognizes customer satisfaction, prevention over inspection, continuous improvement, management responsibility and cost of quality. The purpose of monitoring and evaluating quality on projects is thus to ensure that the customer is satisfied with the product/service/result accruing from the project, the project has a process of continuous improvement in place-collecting and learning from lessons, there is evidence that management takes quality seriously and that the cost of quality is reasonable-striking a balance between the cost of conformance and cost of nonconformance.

22.4 An overview of the Quality Movement

It is important for a project monitoring and evaluation practitioner to understand the philosophies underlying quality. The concepts in these philosophies actually provide the framework through which quality is monitored and evaluated on projects. Kerzner (2008) and Evans & Lindsay (2002) trace these philosophies and the following account is based on their work:

(i) The work of Williams Edwards Deming

W Edwards Deming placed great importance and responsibility on management, at the individual and company level, believing management to be responsible for 94% of quality problems. He developed a 14-point plan that can be applied to small or large organizations in the public, private or service sectors. He believed that adoption of, and action on, the fourteen points was a signal that management intended to stay in business. Deming also encouraged a systematic approach to problem solving and promoted the widely known Plan, Do, Check, Act (PDCA) cycle.

List the 14 points in the Deming's 14-point plan to quality improvement. Explain how this plan ties into the PDCA cycle.

(ii) The work of Dr Joseph M Juran

Dr. Juran developed the quality trilogy i.e. quality planning, quality improvement quality control. According to Dr. Juran good quality management requires quality actions to be planned out, improved and controlled. The process achieves control at one level of quality performance, then plans are made to improve the performance on a project by project basis, using specific tools and techniques. This activity eventually achieves breakthrough to an improved level, which is again controlled, to prevent any deterioration.

Dr. Juran believed quality is associated with customer satisfaction and dissatisfaction with the product, and emphasized the necessity for ongoing quality improvement through a succession of small improvement projects carried out throughout the organization. He formulated the ten steps to quality improvement. Dr. Juran concentrated not just on the end customer, but on other external and internal customers. Each person along the chain, from product designer to final user, is a supplier and a customer. In addition, the person will be a process, carrying out some transformation or activity.

 Write down a critique of Juran's 10 steps to quality improvement.

(iii)The work of Armand V Feigenbaum

Armand was the originator of "total quality control", often referred to as total quality. He defined total quality as *"an effective system for integrating quality development, quality maintenance and quality improvement efforts of the various groups within an organization, so as to enable production and service at the most economical levels that allow full customer satisfaction".*

He saw it as a business method and proposed three steps to quality:

- Quality leadership
- Modern quality technology
- Organizational commitment

(iv)The work of Dr. Kaoru Ishikawa

Dr Kaoru Ishikawa made many contributions to quality, the most noteworthy being his total quality view point, companywide quality control, his emphasis on the human side of quality, the Ishikawa diagram and the assembly and use of the *"seven basic tools of quality"*. These tools are:

- Pareto analysis: which are the big problems?
- Cause and effect diagrams: what causes the problems?
- Stratification: how is the data made up?
- Check sheets: how often it occurs or is done?
- Histograms: what do overall variations look like?
- Scatter charts: what are the relationships between factors?
- Process control charts: which variations to control and how?

He believed these seven tools should be known widely, if not by everyone, in an organization and used to analyze problems and develop improvements. One of the most widely known of these is the Ishikawa (or fishbone or cause and effect) diagram.

Because these tools are the centre of quality monitoring and evaluation, we will explain them in detail later in this lecture.

(v) The work of Dr. Genichi Taguchi

Dr. Genichi Taguchi believed it is preferable to design product that is robust or insensitive to variation in the manufacturing process, rather than attempt to control all the many variations during actual manufacture. To put this idea into practice, he took the already established knowledge on experimental design and made it more usable and practical for quality professionals. His message was concerned with the routine optimization of product and process prior to manufacture rather than quality through inspection. Quality and reliability are pushed back to the design stage where they really belong, and he broke down off-line quality into three stages:

- System design
- Parameter design

212

- Tolerance design

Explain how the "Taguchi Methodology" of system design, parameter design and tolerance design compares with Quality Function Deployment (QFD).

(vi) The work of Shigeo Shingo

Shigeo Shingo is strongly associated with Just-in-Time manufacturing, and was the inventor of the single minute exchange of die (SMED) system, in which set up times are reduced from hours to minutes, and the Poka-Yoke (mistake proofing) system. In Poka Yoke, defects are examined, the production system stopped and immediate feedback given so that the root causes of the problem may be identified and prevented from occurring again. The addition of a checklist recognizes that humans can forget or make mistakes. He distinguished between "errors", which are inevitable, and "defects", which result when an error reaches a customer, and the aim of Poka-Yoke is to stop errors becoming defects. Defects arise because errors are made and there is a cause and effect relationship between the two. Zero quality control is the ideal production system and this requires both Poka-Yoke and source inspections. In the latter, errors are looked at before they become defects, and the system is either stopped for correction or the error condition automatically adjusted to prevent it from becoming a defect.

(vii) The work of Philip B Crosby

Philip B Crosby is known for the concepts of "Quality is Free" and "Zero Defects", and his quality improvement process is based on his four absolutes of quality:

• Quality is conformance to requirements

• The system of quality is prevention. Prevention implies keeping errors out of the process. This is different from inspection which is meant to keep errors out of the hands of the customer.

213

• The performance standard is zero defects

• The measurement of quality is the price of non-conformance

(viii) The work of Tom Peters

Tom Peters identified leadership as being central to the quality improvement process, discarding the word "Management" for "Leadership". The new role is of a facilitator, and the basis is "Managing By Walking Around" (MBWA), enabling the leader to keep in touch with customers, innovation and people, the three main areas in the pursuit of excellence. He believes that, as the effective leader walks, at least 3 major activities are happening:

• Listening suggests caring

• Teaching values are transmitted

• Facilitating able to give on-the-spot help

MBWA based interventions have been shown to lead to improved achievement of healthcare goals (Anita, L.T.& Sara, J. S., 2013).

Your host institution is a large county hospital. The hospital board is concerned that they are not meeting targets particularly in both their front and back office operations. You believe that implementing MBWA intervention will reverse the trends. Draft a one-page board paper explaining how MBWA can be implemented at

22.5 Quality Assurance and Control

Quality assurance is the collective term for the formal activities and managerial processes that attempt to ensure that products and services meet the required quality level. Quality assurance also includes efforts internal and external to these assurance function that attempt to ensure that the project scope, cost, and time functions are fully integrated. Quality assurance is the management section of quality management. This is the area where the project manager needs to establish the administrative processes and procedures necessary to ensure and, often, prove that the scope statement conforms to the actual requirement of the customer. All relevant legal and regulatory requirements must also be met. According to Kerzner (2008), a good quality assurance system will:

- Identify objectives and standards
- Be multifunctional and prevention oriented.
- Plan for collection and use of data in a cycle of continuous improvement.
- Plan for the establishment and maintenance of performance measures

Include quality audits. A quality audit is an independent evaluation performed by qualified quality personnel that ensures that the project is conforming to the project's quality requirements and is following the established quality procedures and policies.

 State any 5 qualities of a good project quality audit

Quality control involves the process of monitoring and recording results to assess performance and recommend necessary changes (*PMBOK® Guide* (2013). It is a collective term for the activities and techniques, within the process, that are intended to create specific quality characteristics. Such activities include continually monitoring processes, identifying and eliminating problem causes, use of statistical process control to reduce the variability and to increase the efficiency process. Quality control certifies that the organization's quality objectives are being met. Quality control is the technical aspect of quality management. According to Kerzner (2008), a good quality control system will:

- Select who to control.
- Set standards that provide the basis for decision regarding the possible corrective action.

215

- Establish the measurement methods used.
- Compare the actual results to the quality standards.
- Act to bring nonconforming processes and material back to standards based on the information collected.
- Monitor and calibrate measuring devices
- Include detailed document for all processes.

 Cost of quality is usually divided into two: conformance and non conformance costs. Can you list down the components of each of these cost categories?

Quality assurance and control generally utilize what Dr Kaoru Ishikawa called the "Seven basic quality tools". Kerzner (2008) and the *PMBOK® Guide* (2013) provide a detailed analysis of these tools.

(i) Data Tables (Stratification or Check sheets)

Data tables, or data arrays, provide a systematic method for data collection and display. They stratify data to show how that data is made up. In most cases, data tables are forms designed for the purpose of collecting specific data. They provide a consistent, effective, and economic approach to gathering data, organizing them for analysis and displaying them for preliminary review. Data tables sometimes take the form of manual check sheets where automated data are not necessary or available.

Illustrate how you can use data tables to monitor supplier quality on projects.

(ii) Cause and effect analysis

After identifying a problem, it is necessary to determine its cause. A considerable amount of analysis is often required to determine the specific cause or causes of the problem. Cause-effect analysis uses diagramming techniques to identify the relationship between the effects and causes. Case-effect diagrams are also known as fishbone diagrams or Ishikawa diagrams. Kerzner (2008) recommends a six-step approach to perform a cause-effect analysis. These are:

- Step 1: Identify the problem
- Step 2: Select interdisciplinary brainstorming team
- Step 3: Draw problem box and prime arrow
- Step 4: Specify major categories of the causes of the problem
- Step 5: Identify defect cause
- Step 6: Identify corrective action

An example Ishikawa diagram is shown below for the project involving fighting the HIV/AIDS scourge. In the example, the problem has been identified as non-achievement of one or more indicators on a project and causes are categorized as:

- Prevention with positives (PPs)
- Counselling and testing targeting general population (CT GP)
- Counselling and testing targeting Most at Risk Populations (CT MARPS)
- Home and community based care (HCBC)
- Behaviour Change Communication targeting youth (BCC Youth)
- Behaviour change communication targeting most at risk populations (BCC MARPS)
- Behaviour change communication targeting fisher forks (BCC FF)

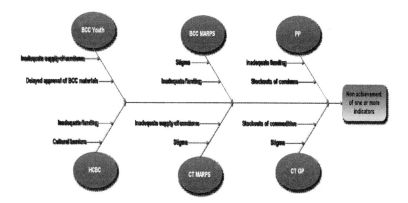

Figure 22.1: Ishikawa diagram for the project involving fighting the HIV/AIDS scourge

(iii)Histogram.

A histogram is a graphical representation of data as a frequency distribution. This tool is valuable in evaluating both attribute (pass/fail) and variable (measurement) data. Histograms offer a quick look at the data at a single point in time; they do not display variance or trends over time. A histogram displays how the cumulative data look today. It is useful in understanding the relative frequencies (percentages) or frequency (numbers) of the data and how those data are distributed (Kerzner, 2008).

(iv)   **Pareto Analysis**

A Pareto diagram is a special type of histogram that helps us to identify and prioritize problem areas. It is for this reason that Pareto analysis is also referred to as the *Rule of the vital few*. The construction of a Pareto diagram may involve data collected from data figures, maintenance data, repair data; parts scrap rates or other sources. By identifying types of nonconformity from any of these data sources, the Pareto diagram directs attention to the most frequently occurring element. Kerzner (2008) identifies three uses and types of Pareto analysis to be:

218

- The basic Pareto analysis identifies the vital few contributors that account for the most quality problems in any system. The basic Pareto analysis chart provides an evaluation of the most frequent occurrences for any given data sets.
- The comparative Pareto analysis focuses on any number of programs options and actions.
- The weighted Pareto analysis gives a measure of significance to factors that may not appear significant at first- such additional factors as cost, time, and criticality.

An example of this basic Pareto analysis is shown in the table below. It is used to quantify and to graph the frequencies of occurrence for material receipt and inspection and further identifies the most significant, based on frequency.

Pareto analysis diagrams are also used to determine the effect of corrective action or to analyze the differences between two or more processes and methods. For a deeper understanding of Pareto Charts refer to Kerzner (2008).

BATCH RECEIPT AND INSPECTION FREQUENCY OF FAILURES			
BATCH	FAILING FREQUENCY	PERCENT FAILING	CUMULATIVE PERCENT
1	13	38	38
2	6	17	55
3	7	20	75
4	9	25	100

Table 22.1: Example of Pareto Analysis

(v) Scatter Diagrams

A scatter diagram organizes data using two variables: an independent and a dependent variable. These data are recorded on a simple graph with X and Y coordinates showing the relationship between the variables. From these scatter diagrams we can develop a trend. Trend analysis is a statistical method for determining the equation that best fits the data in the scatter plot.

Trend analysis quantifies the relationship of the data, determines the equation, and measures the fit equation to the data. This method is also known as curve fitting or least squares. Trend analysis can determine optimal operating conditions by providing an equation that describes the relationship between the dependent (output) and independent (input) variables. Run Charts are used to plot data/change along a timeline.

(vi) Control Charts (Shewart charts)

The use of control charts focuses on the prevention of defects, rather than their detection and rejection. In business, government, and industry, economy and efficiency is always best saved by prevention. It costs much more to produce an unsatisfactory product or services than it does to produce a satisfactory one. The construction, use and interpretation of control charts is based on the normal statistical distribution. The center line of the control chart represents the average or the mean of the data (X).The upper and lower control limits (UCL and LCL), respectively, represent this plus and minus three standard deviations of the data. ($X \pm 3s$). Control limits identify the boundaries of common variation in a statistically stable process or process performance. This is different from tolerances which are specified ranges of acceptable results. Either the lower case s or Greek letter σ (sigma) represents the standard deviation of the control charts. The normal distribution can be described entirely by its mean and standard deviation. The normal distribution is a bell-shaped curve.(sometime called the Gaussian distribution) that is symmetrical about the mean, slopes downward on both sides to infinity, and theoretically has an infinite range.

In normal distribution 99.73% of all measurements lie within X+3s and X-3s, this is why the limits on control charts are called three-sigma limits. Companies like Motorola have embarked upon a six-sigma limit rather than a three sigma limit. Control chart analysis determines whether the inherent process variability and the process average are at stable levels, whether one or both are out of statistical control (not stable), or whether appropriate action needs to be taken. Another purpose of using control charts is to distinguish between the inherent, random variability of a process and the variability attributed to an assignable cause. The sources of random variability are often referred to as common causes. These are the sources that cannot be changed readily, without significant restructuring of the process. Common cause variability or variation is a source of random variation that is always present in any process. It is that part of the variability inherent in the process itself. The cause of this variation can be corrected only by a management decision to change the basic process.

Special cause (assignable cause) variability, by contrast, is subject to correction within the process under process control. This variation can be controlled at the local or operational level. Special causes are indicated by a point on the control chart that is beyond the control limit or by a persistent trend approaching the control limit. To use process control measurements data effectively, it is important to understand the concept of variation.

The factors that cause the most variability in the process are the main factors found on cause-and-effect analysis charts such as people, machines, methodology, materials, measurements and environment. There are two types of control charts: variable charts for use with continuous data and attribute charts for use with the discrete data.

(vi) Flow Charts

These are also referred to as process maps since they display the sequence of steps and the branching possibilities that exist for a process that transforms one or more inputs into one or more outputs. They show the activities, decision points, branching loops, parallel paths and the overall order of processing by mapping the operational details of procedures that exist within a horizontal value chain of the Supplier-Input-Process-Output-Customer (SIPOC) model. Flowcharts are helpful in estimating the cost of quality in a process by using the workflow branching logic and associated relative frequencies to estimate expected monetary value for the conformance and nonconformance work required to deliver the expected conforming output.

221

22.6 Acceptance Sampling

Acceptance sampling is a process of evaluating a portion of a lot for the purpose of accepting or rejecting the entire lot. Determination of whether to accept or reject a lot is often called lot sentencing and this is the true purpose of acceptance sampling (Evans & Lindsay, 2002). It is an attempt to monitor the quality of the incoming product or material after completion of production. The alternative to developing a sampling plan would be 100% inspection. The costs associated with 100% are prohibitive, and the risks associated with 0% inspection are likewise large. Therefore, some sort of compromise is needed. The three most commonly used sampling plans are:

- Single sampling: This is the acceptance or rejection of a lot based upon one sampling run.
- Double sampling: A small sample size is tested. If the results are not conclusive, then second sample is tested.
- Multiple sampling: This process requires the sampling of several small lots.

Regardless of what type of sampling plan is chosen, sampling errors can occur. A shipment of good-quality items can be rejected if a large portion of defective units are selected at random. Likewise, a bad-quality shipment can be accepted if the tested sample contains disproportionately large numbers of quality items. The two major risks are:

- Producer's risks: This is called the α (alpha) risk or type I error. This is the risk to the producer that a good lot will be rejected.
- Consumer's risk: This is called the β (beta) risk or type II error. This is the consumer's risk of accepting a bad lot.

When a lot is tested for quality, we can look at either "attribute" or "variable" quality data. Attribute quality data are either quantitative or qualitative data for which the product or service is designed and built. Variable quality data are quantitative, continuous measurement processes to either accept or reject a lot. The exact measurements can be either destructive or nondestructive testing.

222

22.7 Summary

We have now come to the end of this lecture. In this lecture, we explained the concept of project quality management and traced the quality movement to enable you develop a framework of monitoring and evaluating quality on projects. We then explained the distinction between quality assurance and quality control. We have also discussed the quality assurance and control tools. Finally, we have presented the rationale for

22.8 Self-test

1. Compare the Six-Sigma DMAIC with the Deming PDCA models of quality management.

2. Explain the factors that you need to consider before implementing either of these models in any organization.

22.9 Suggestions for further reading

Anita, L. T. & Sara, J. S. (2013).*The Effectiveness of Management-By-Walking-Around: A Randomized Field Study. Harvard Business School.*

Evans, J.R. & Lindsay, W.M. (2002).*THE MANAGEMENT AND CONTROL OF QUALITY* (5th edition). Cincinnati, Ohio: South-Western, Thomson Learning.

Kerzner, H. (2008), *Project Management-A Systems Approach to Planning, Scheduling, and Controlling*(10th Edition). John Wiley & Sons Inc.

Project Management Institute, (2013), *A Guide to the Project Management Body of Knowledge (*5th ed.).Newton Square, PA: Author.

LECTURES TWENTY-THREE, TWENTY FOUR & TWENTY-FIVE: GUIDED FIELDWORK-PERFORMANCE ASSESSMENT AND RISK EVALUATION OF A LIVE PROJECT

Lecture Outline

Select one project as a class (either ongoing or completed but large enough to enable learning). Develop a checklist/questionnaire to enable you collect data necessary to evaluate this project on the basis of:

- Efficiency
- Effectiveness
- Economy
- Relevance
- Risk
- Sustainability
- Learning

Using the developed checklist/questionnaire, proceed to collect data on this project. Analyze these data and make appropriate recommendations. complete the evaluation report and prepare power point slides for presentation of the findings and recommendations to the stakeholders.

LECTURE TWENTY-SIX: PRESENTATION OF PERFORMANCE ASSESSMENT AND RISK EVALUATION REPORT

Lecture Outline

Using the power point presentation you developed, present your findings and recommendations to the stakeholders' forum (this can be a class or actual project stakeholders) to obtain feedback and sign off. In your presentation, identify any challenges you encountered in conducting the evaluation and explain how you went about those challenges. Using the feedback obtained during the presentation, compile the final report for the evaluation.

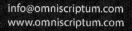

Printed in Great Britain
by Amazon

70038060R00139